Becoming the Teacher You Wish You'd Had

I have trained future teachers for nineteen years, and this work is by far the best book on teaching I have put in their hands. My methods students tell me that this book both inspires them and makes them aware of the incredible challenges they will face in their future classrooms. They universally call it the best book they have been assigned in their education classes.

—Jeff Gall, PhD, Professor of History and Social Science Education,
Truman State University

I have read countless books on education, pedagogy, and leadership during my career, most of the time slogging through them looking for the pearls of wisdom, insight, and inspiration that I could use in my leadership life. I always enjoy and benefit the most from a practitioner's point of view—someone who actually put the philosophy, principles, ideas, and values into practice. This author's perspective on great teaching has credibility and high value because he is a lifetime teacher—a master of the craft of teaching who won the trust, admiration, and respect of students and colleagues. When you add his gift of communication that includes wit, humor, humility, and Scott Holley hyperbole, along with very pointed, well-positioned quotes, you end up with a book that is as entertaining as it is inspirational—not an easy objective to fulfill.

—Jim Marsh, Director of the Van Lunen Center, Calvin College

Accessible, heartwarming, and genuine, this book lays out the essential fundamentals of teaching in a way that flows easily and passionately. The author gives the reader a set of comprehensive building blocks, and leaves us believing we can build a pyramid. His writing is infused with a wisdom that is both theoretical and practical, that lives simultaneously in the big picture and the smallest details, and moves effortlessly between the two. Part memoir, part self-help book, the author's own experiences and teachings are enhanced by a chorus of other thoughtfully placed voices and framed by a series of stimulating questions that function as both an invitation and a call to action. I believe I am a better tutor and overall human being after reading this book.

—Jacqueline Thornton, academic consultant

Becoming the
TEACHER
You Wish You'd Had

A CONVERSATION ABOUT TEACHING

SCOTT HOLLEY

Education and the Liberal Arts
Truman State University Press
Kirksville, Missouri

Copyright © 2017 Scott Holley/Truman State University Press, Kirksville, Missouri, 63501
All rights reserved
tsup.truman.edu

Cover art: school books and apple against blackboard, Shutterstock ID# 352382909, ©ampcool, used with permission; rubbed out on blackboard, Shutterstock ID#111463604, ©STILLFX, used with permission.
Cover design: Lisa Ahrens

Library of Congress Cataloging-in-Publication Data

Names: Holley, Scott, author.
Title: Becoming the teacher you wish you'd had : a conversation about teaching / by Scott Holley.
Description: Kirksville, Missouri : Truman State University Press, [2016] | Series: Education and liberal arts | Includes bibliographical references and index.
Identifiers: LCCN 2017001144 (print) | LCCN 2017010230 (ebook) | ISBN 9781612481906 (pbk. : alk. paper) | ISBN 9781612481913
Subjects: LCSH: Teaching. | Teachers. | Teacher-student relationships.
Classification: LCC LB1025.3 .H634 2016 (print) | LCC LB1025.3 (ebook) | DDC 371.102—dc23
LC record available at https://lccn.loc.gov/2017001144

To Joan, whose love, support, kindness, and faith have made all the difference.

Contents

Chapter Nine: Assessments That Make a Difference 167

Chapter Ten: Conclusion 188

Endnotes 197

Works Cited 201

About the Author 207

Acknowledgments

Any book about education is a partnership, a collaboration forged through the relationships that shape a teacher's pedagogy, philosophy, and values, so the words that follow are written to express my gratitude to the administrators, teachers, students, friends, and family who helped me define what it means to devote my entire career to trying to figure out what teaching and learning are really about. If Cecil Nettles and Don Senti had not taken a chance on a young man who had little idea of what to do in the classroom, I would never have had the opportunity to work through the struggles of those first few years to achieve any level of maturity as a teacher. If Patrick Berger had not taken me on as one of his many projects and given me the chance to work in collaboration with him, I never would have gained the confidence to know that I could actually connect with kids about serious, far-ranging ideas. If I had not worked in a department with such educators as Jim Schmuck, Mike Hopkins, Barb Harris, Ann Brown, Becky Pearce, and Nick Otten, I would never have known that teachers could challenge each other to get better and better while having so much fun. These are the men and women who influenced my early years as a teacher, the men and women from whom I learned so much and whose wisdom echoed in my head for the rest of my career.

The list of key influencers only grew exponentially once I left that school for another. Bob Vass, Betsy Tyvoll, Larry Birchler, Florence Lewis, Andrew Shaw, Lucy Erdman, Ken Boesch, Mike Parker, Sue Tameling, Chris Knerr, Kathy Karigan, Chris Pederson, Cory Snyder, Susie Brown, Scott VonderBruegge, Ann Heyse, L. B. Graham, Sherry Blough, Jill Keith, Tim Baldwin, among many others, are all educators who in different ways loved their students, served them well, and set an example for me to follow. Working with each was a joy, and by learning from them, I became a better teacher and a better person. Special mention must go to Cindy Zavaglia, who helped to give me a higher vision of what a school working in community could and should be and who influenced our school (and me) in ways both profound and far-reaching. Seeing young teachers like Micah Gall, Nicole Scholten, Heather Marsee, Dan Burke, Mallory Rohlfing, Nick Gray, Allison Pautler, and Gina Butterfield sink their roots deeply into the classroom enriched my final years. Knowing that the next generation will be served by men and women of such commitment, talent, and wisdom gives me great hope for tomorrow. And many thanks too for the dozens of other teachers with whom I shared a conversation about teaching; I took something meaningful away from each of those encounters, and I became a better teacher because of it.

The years spent in administration with men like Jim Sefrit, Tim Hall, and Steve Hall were the highlight of my career. Whether we were laughing together or dealing with the most serious issues imaginable, I treasured my time with them and still value the lessons they taught me. Just when I thought I had the answer, one of them would share a perspective that reminded me once again that wisdom comes through shared counsel and good friendship. And no words can express the respect I have for Jim Marsh, about whom these words say it all: he is one of the few truly great men I have ever known.

Trying to name the students who helped to form my understanding of what good teaching looks like is impossible. Every student posed a different opportunity and challenge, and trying to figure out how to motivate this one or how to encourage that one was a pedagogical puzzle that never failed to engage my energies and attention. But so many students were a joy to teach, and witnessing their offbeat humor, their efforts to make sense of a perplexing passage of literature, and their awakening sense of their own abilities was a privilege.

Many other voices helped to shape this book. Listening to Lou Jobst speak of his love for his students was moving, hearing Randy Pearce talk with passion and humor about guiding his students toward confidence in debate, and sitting with Dave Shapleigh on the last day of his career as he reflected on the joy he found in the classroom were powerful testaments to their love of teaching. Seeing the humility of

Earl Hopper emerge as he spoke about his years as a teacher and coach was a reminder of just how much good teachers care about their students. Jeff Gall's encouragement throughout the process of writing this book was of more value than he will ever know. Every time I got discouraged and wondered if this book had any value his voice would provide the boost I needed to keep going. If ever a writer had a champion, he was it. Matthew Arkin and Meghan Pinson offered excellent editorial advice and made the manuscript much better than it would have been had I not benefited from their counsel.

The contributions of my brothers cannot possibly be overstated. Throughout my career I enjoyed talking shop with David and Mike, whose contributions to education dwarf my own. They were great teachers, and the number of students who would say that one of them was his best teacher ever is countless. Tom was the only brother of the four not to go into education, but the entire family knows how he has blessed all of us, and it is safe to say that we would not have been the teachers we were without his efforts. His generosity and example are well known throughout the entire community.

Tim, Jeff, and Jill, my children, are the ones who taught me the most about teaching. From them I learned the value of patience, of not giving up, of extending grace, of drawing lines where they need to be drawn, and most of all, the importance of love in any relationship that seeks to shape a life. I am proud of each of them, love them dearly, and am so grateful that they have become the men and woman they have become. Thanks too for Rex, Amy, and Sarah for joining our family and loving our children and grandchildren well. As for Joan—she walked through almost all of the forty-one-year journey with me, consoling me when things went poorly, encouraging me when the students didn't get it, celebrating our successes, sitting in the bleachers at far too many basketball games or track meets, tolerating the hours and hours I spent grading, and loving me so well. She has shaped my life in ways I am not even aware of, and no man could take as much satisfaction as I do in knowing that his wife has been the greatest blessing of his life. Thanks to you most of all.

Introduction

I am a teacher, a man whose desire to teach is rooted in his blood. My paternal grandmother graduated from the first class ever at what is now Missouri State University and taught for several years before starting a family. My mother volunteered with one of the first high school programs in the Midwest for students with special needs. My older brother was a history teacher for more than fifteen years and a principal for another twenty. My younger brother was a middle school and high school history teacher for most of his career, my son is a teacher, my nephew is a teacher, and my niece is a teacher. The tally of kids who have sat in the classroom under the care of a member of my family numbers in the thousands since collectively we have spent well over one hundred years in education. Teaching is what we do, it is what we know, it is who we are.

But for me, the road to competence in the classroom was a painstaking, sometimes embarrassing ordeal that seemed destined for disaster in the early years as I struggled with my own insecurity, immaturity, and ineffectiveness. The lessons I learned on the path toward understanding how to teach came slowly, painfully, and at great cost to my pride as I wrestled with the thought that I might fail absolutely at achieving the dream I had always wanted to pursue.

That's because from the time my ineptitude at the plate and in the field forced me to abandon my childhood fantasy of playing centerfield for the St. Louis Cardinals, my sole ambition became much more modest—though fundamentally far more important. I dreamed of walking into a classroom filled with adolescents and helping them to discover beauty in the power of ideas. I remember clearly the day I decided to teach—a cold December day in Mrs.

Wilson's sixth-grade class circa 1962 in Kirkwood, Missouri. As the quiet buzz of the radiator hummed to my left and the frosted glass glazed by the winter chill sparkled to my right, my classmates and I sat quietly at our desks reading a story that absolutely riveted me. Something about the power of that story and the cozy warmth of that scene touched my naïve twelve-year-old soul. I felt at home in the classroom, at home engaging with ideas and finding a haven where learning was taken seriously. Captured by that moment, I put down my book, took a deep breath, and made a decision that day that I never relinquished—I was going to become a teacher. And despite a less than focused academic career, an uneven student teaching experience, and the rockiest start imaginable, I never wavered from that goal.

That was more than fifty years ago. In the ensuing years, I taught English in public schools, private schools, and international schools. I taught seventh graders, eighth graders, freshmen, juniors, and seniors, but somehow never managed to teach a class of sophomores. Little by little I learned how to teach, and though I never mastered the craft, I learned to love it. Being with teenagers all day long filled me with joy, gave me a hopeful perspective on the next generation that my more cynical friends in the adult world did not share, and allowed me to go to work each day knowing that what I did mattered.

I remember a conversation I had with four friends, all about my age, at a New Year's Eve party as we celebrated the coming of the new millennium. Each of these men made far more money than I did. Each held a senior position in his company and was highly regarded as a man of both integrity and ability. Yet as we talked about our jobs, they all expressed a sense of frustration that although their work was intellectually engaging and financially rewarding, none of them found any real meaning in what he did all day long. One of them said something I will never forget: "Life has to be about more than watching interest rates go up and down." Whatever the frustrations of the classroom, I have never doubted that what happens in it makes a difference. Though I had plenty of days in which I didn't really connect with the kids and faced more than a few disengaged students, I knew that the lives of these kids mattered a heck of a lot more than the fluctuations of the prime lending rate.

I was blessed to be a teacher. And because I loved it so much, I have thought a lot about what it means to teach, how to think about what to teach, and how to improve as a teacher. The truth is that no one ever arrives as a teacher; no matter how good we may be, we all have wretched days in which our carefully crafted lessons fall apart, and we all have distant students with whom we never seem to connect. On occasion I would get in the car after a string of less than stellar classes knowing that I did not earn my salary that day. But the beauty of being a teacher is that, like the outfielder who goes 0 for 4 and leaves five men on base during Monday's game, Tuesday brings another chance to step into the box to have a go at redemption. And that's what I tried to do for forty-one years.

This book is an exploration of the art and craft of teaching—not from an academic but from a practitioner who struggled and failed and experimented and grew, and who never quit aiming to get better. Teaching humbled me. The kids humbled me. In a job interview for a new position a few years ago, someone asked me to explain my teaching style and was clearly distressed when I replied, "I don't know." He kept pressing, asking me to define what a typical day in my class looked like, and my insistence that I couldn't define a typical day unsettled him; in his eyes, I was evidently an amateurish fraud who had no understanding of the science of teaching and could not be trusted to provide the students with a rigorous education grounded in sound practice. But to me each day is a work in progress, and what dazzles on Wednesday might bomb on Thursday. What soars during third hour might not fly during sixth. A good teacher is a jazz impresario adapting on the fly as he or she gauges the kids' body language and responsiveness. Because no two groups of students are alike, and no two students are either, a good teacher must learn to change the tempo moment by moment or engage in a spontaneous riff that takes the class to places he or she did not anticipate when the bell rang at the beginning of class. If I have an undergirding pedagogical approach it is this: *Whatever it takes.* Though I had (and have) strong beliefs about what and why teachers should teach, my attitudes about how they do it were (and are) more flexible. But I do know this: Good teachers cannot be so rigid in their approach that they plunge blindly through a lesson as the kids descend into zombieland. After all, the classroom is for the kids, not the teacher.

What follows is an examination of what one man believes about teaching kids in middle school and high school. Actually, that is not entirely true. What follows is the end result of more than forty years of reflecting upon, reading about, and practicing the art and science of teaching, all enhanced by the perspectives of many other voices, some of them educational experts like Linda Darling-Hammond and Grant Wiggins and Robert Marzano, and some of them career teachers like me. Throughout my years in education, I liked to sit with other master teachers, both in my own building and beyond, to pick their brains, whether in a formal interview or in a casual conversation, about what they had learned; some of what follows represents their wisdom, their experience, their counsel. More recently I sat with a number of men and women newly retired from the field and interviewed them about what they've learned in their many years in the classroom. Some of them had taught for more than forty years; the least experienced left the classroom after "only" twenty-four years. These men and women were masters of their craft, the kind of educators that every school longs to hire and every parent prays will teach their children. It has always seemed wrong that on the day teachers retire, they walk out the door taking all of their years of practice and planning and preparation with them; the younger teachers they leave behind will never benefit from their hard-earned expertise. This book—a mix of philosophy, memoir, and practical advice—is meant to correct that reality by offering a series of reflections from those who have spent years in the profession or years studying it. This discussion of what works and what does not, what matters and what can be put aside, is directed at teachers who are striving, at any stage in their career, to master the never-ending challenge of facing a roomful of teenagers and somehow making what we do matter to them and, more importantly, helping them to become more literate, more thoughtful, and more humane. To say that this book will provide a roadmap for success in the classroom is more than I can claim. But to borrow a phrase from Peter King's Monday Morning Quarterback column for *Sports Illustrated*, the thoughts below are "Things I Think I Think" about what defines great teaching.

I never got it right. I never ended a school year without regrets that I had failed this student or misunderstood that one. One of my very last acts in my final days as a teacher was to flunk a student I could never reach. Yet I was not the same teacher in my last year that I was in my first, largely because I had taught with and learned from many, many great teachers. To walk away without reflecting once more on what they taught me and what I figured out about how to reach a group of sometimes reluctant learners seems a terrible waste. To claim that I am an expert qualified to offer general advice on how to teach seems more than a little pretentious; many people with whom I have worked could do it as well or even better. And to suggest that I can offer any revolutionary insight into how best to teach is wishful thinking since so much of what makes a teacher successful is simply common sense. I love Fran Lebowitz's words: "Original thought is like original sin: both happened before you were born to people you could not possibly have met."[1] Little of what follows will be new, earth-shattering, or profound. But if forty-one years in the classroom taught me anything, if the wisdom of those who conduct educational research means anything, and if the perspectives of the men and women I interviewed for this book count for anything at all, it is that much of what we've managed to discover about how to reach kids was learned painfully and slowly but ultimately led to a career filled with purpose, excitement, and even joy. If any of the reflections that follow shorten the learning curve for young teachers trying to figure it out, if anything that follows helps them to see that though our tools and priorities may change, the need for thoughtful reflection does not, then these thoughts may be of value. For what it is worth, this is what I have learned.

Chapter One
First Year Follies

I wish I could say that my transition to the classroom was a joyful exercise in creative lesson plans, innovative teaching strategies, and hosannas from grateful students carrying me on their shoulders from the classroom to my car each Friday at 3:15 as they exulted in the brilliance of the insights they had gained each week. I wish I could say that every Monday morning appreciative parents lined the hallways outside my classroom shedding tears of joy and pressing oversized wads of cash into my hands as they thanked me for the life-changing experience their children were having because of my class. The reality was just a tad different.

My first year in teaching was, in fact, little short of a nightmare: two semesters of self-doubt, second-guessing, and sleepless nights spent ruing my inability to command the attention and respect of the students, who seemed far more adept at running the class than I was. My career began in the early 1970s in a rural community that was transitioning to suburbia as the sprawl of St. Louis spread southward. I was hired to teach seventh- and eighth-grade English to the children of families for whom aspirations of a college education were a novelty since their children were primed to return to the farm or find work at the nearby Chrysler plant that seemed to employ half of their fathers. The school was proudly old-fashioned, with corporal punishment the preferred method of classroom management and a curriculum little changed since the 1950s. Apart from student teaching and the usual round of education classes that were part of my undergraduate coursework, my preparation for my new assignment was nonexistent. I reported two days before school began and was handed my textbooks, given a whirlwind blast of school policies and procedures, and sent on my way with the hope that I was at least moderately competent. I was not.

In an effort to be innovative, the principal paired me for two periods a day with a sixty-seven-year-old veteran who was in her last year of teaching. Mrs. Dwight (not her real name) had been teaching since the Great Depression and had absolutely no interest in listening to the half-baked ideas of a novice who had no real idea how to teach anyway. Our pairing was not exactly a rousing success. Mrs. Dwight's preferred method of instruction was a lecture followed by worksheets—day after day after day. Whatever creative ideas I might have had were ignored, which, given her experience and my naiveté, made perfect sense. We were assigned to a classroom that had once been the school library, which meant we had a cavernous space in which to operate. Given all of that room, the principal decided to fill it with as many twelve- and thirteen-year-olds as he possibly could, so we had between sixty and seventy kids in each of the two periods we team-taught. It was not his best idea.

Try to picture the scene: Mrs. Dwight and I took turns lecturing on the glories of the parts of speech, topic sentences, and dangling modifiers while a small horde of seventh graders sat slack-jawed in disbelief at the sheer lunacy of what we were doing. Whether due to age or lack of interest, Mrs. Dwight never bothered to learn the students' names, nor did she ever know who among the kids could be trusted and who needed to be watched, which set her up for embarrassment on more than one occasion. Lisa* was both the best student in the entire seventh grade and among the kindest girls I ever taught in my entire career. She thanked me every single day as she left class, even as I stood at the door lowering my eyes in shame at the utter irrelevance of what we had just forced the students to endure. Bored beyond even her superhuman tolerance for putting up with information she had known since she was eight, Lisa was reading a book one March day as Mrs. Dwight droned on and on about the glories of adverbs and adjectives. Catching sight of Lisa's inattention, Mrs. Dwight called her to the board in a furious tone to circle every adjective and adverb in a lengthy passage from Ernest Gaines's *The Autobiography of Miss Jane Pittman*. I knew what was going to happen, the class knew what was going to happen, and, to Lisa's credit, she did too. Lisa looked my way, silently imploring me to somehow short-circuit this whole charade. Not knowing how to rescue Mrs. Dwight or Lisa, I shrugged as Lisa dragged herself to the board with the greatest reluctance and completed the task in record time, sending the entire class into titters of delight at the sight of Mrs. Dwight sputtering in humiliation by her desk.

Mrs. Dwight also had a complete aversion to handling discipline problems, which in a room full of three score or more seventh graders, were an ever-present threat and an all-too-common reality. Her response to any and all disruptions was to stand by the mischief-maker with her hands on her hips as her lower lip trembled like a low-level earthquake. She would grunt loudly, sounding like a cross between a badly tuned engine and a grizzly bear emerging from hibernation, which was intended to signal that trouble was afoot and my services were required. So though I might be on the far side of the room and rarely had any idea what had just happened, I was expected to be the dutiful sheriff riding in to restore order. I would rush to her side as her lip quivered frantically and the grunting escalated, not knowing if I was being summoned because someone had just dropped his pencil on the floor or had hijacked a 747. She would point in horror at the offender, directing me to take him out into the hall to launch an interrogation worthy of a John Grisham courtroom thriller to ferret out the truth of the offense.

One day this scenario went horribly wrong. Intent on helping a struggling student near the front of the room write an acceptable topic sentence, I was startled to hear Mrs. Dwight's badly tuned engine and comatose bear awaken with unprecedented volume. I scurried to the back of the room to do my duty, but this time the script unraveled quickly. Rather than playing his part and quietly retreating to the hall for his interrogation, this young man jumped to his feet and fled my attempts to nab him.

I should have let him go. I should have recognized this was a situation that could not possibly end with anyone escaping with any dignity whatsoever. But I was twenty-two years old, immature, inexperienced, and propelled by the escalating cacophony of Mrs. Dwight's grunts, so I took off in hot pursuit, chasing him up and down the rows of the classroom as the other students reveled in the spectacle of their teacher making a complete fool of himself. The chase seemed interminable as he scattered empty desks in my path in his effort to flee and ended only when a sympathetic girl blocked his escape with her desk, allowing me to corral him so that I could drag him into custody in the hallway. Out of breath and poised for the kill, I bored in to uncover the truth of his heinous offense. Furious that he had been caught, the boy was reluctant to come clean, but he finally caved, telling me that he had committed a truly unspeakable crime: he had forgotten to bring his pencil to class.

My other three classes weren't much better. Each was filled with thirty or more eighth graders skilled in smelling the weakness of a new teacher, and I gave them every opportunity to draw blood. Trying too hard to be liked, I set a much too casual tone in the class, and when the kids sensed I was an easy mark, they took full advantage. Pulling out the full arsenal of early adolescent foolishness, the kids specialized in high caliber spit wad wars, passed notes with the efficiency of UPS during the Christmas rush, and chattered on as I tried to teach as if I were the Invisible Man. My days were filled with classroom chaos and my nights with constant grading and frenzied efforts to stay a few days ahead of the kids in planning each week's lessons.

By October I was exhausted, wanting desperately to hit the reset button so I could create a new classroom atmosphere, but the relentless pace of the calendar meant I had to hang on until Christmas when I might have sufficient time to get far enough ahead to actually generate lessons that would appeal to the students. I had no social life, no life apart from school. Still single, I was zero for the school year on the dating scene because I spent every moment outside the classroom trying to figure out how to reach these kids who seemed to have such little interest in learning. My friends thought I had been swallowed by a black hole. Never had I been so stripped of my dignity. Never had I felt like such a failure. Lying awake late at night, I would wonder how it was possible that I had wanted so badly to teach for so long yet could be so inept. If I could have quit without suffering a fatal blow to my pride, I would have done so but instead chose to grind through the bedlam simply because I felt I had no option. Though there might have been veteran teachers in the building willing to help, I was so cowed by my daily struggles that I hesitated to go to them because I did not want anyone to know the depths of my struggles, and no one ever approached me to offer any advice. Year one was a long slog filled with insecurity, long hours, and, at my worst moments, despair.

But I hung in. Whether motivated by stubborn pride or an unwillingness to let go of a dream so quickly, I just could not allow myself to walk away without taking one more shot. And year two was better. I was granted no sudden epiphany that unlocked the secrets of the classroom, but somehow that second year marked real progress and even moments of genuine delight. Mrs. Dwight retired, and though the ill-conceived team-teaching experiment was shelved, for planning purposes I was paired with two women in their thirties who were more attuned to the students and more willing to work with someone who was inexperienced yet was more than willing to learn. Both were kind, both were young enough to remember just how difficult teaching can be for a beginner, and we worked well together throughout the year, developing assignments with some actual creativity that challenged the students to think in ways that would have never occurred to Mrs. Dwight. By the end of that year, I was far from a polished teacher, but at least I had gained enough confidence and enough street smarts through my colleagues' assistance to think that I might actually make it. I had been badly bloodied, but I was still standing, and the kids actually seemed to have learned something.

If this sad history doesn't make the reality clear, let's state it as plainly as possible: the first few years in the classroom are *hard*. The road to competence—let alone excellence—in the classroom is filled with unimaginable potholes and speed bumps. In years of conversations with veteran teachers, whether the setting was a backyard barbecue, a staff training in-service day, or a formal interview for this book, only one person even dared to suggest that her transition to the classroom was seamless. Given her forceful personality and thoughtful approach to education, I believe it when she says she knew what she was doing on day one of year one. But all of the other teachers I have ever spoken to about their early years take on the countenance of a lapsed Catholic going to confession; they lower their eyes to the ground, drop their head in embarrassment, and tell a sad tale of woe while begging for absolution. Whether their downfall is an unruly group of students, insufficient background in their subject matter, or a lack of understanding of the basic principles of pedagogy, beginning teachers almost universally find themselves facing a bad case of shell shock sometime within the first semester. Once the school year starts, the mistakes pile up and the idealism that rookie teachers bring to the table is put to the test almost immediately. The obstacles new teachers face are common and predictable, roadblocks that make that first year a march of folly bearable only because the beacon of summer vacation looms on the far horizon and the promise that with practice things will improve. Here are at least some of the major barriers many young teachers face as they seek to acclimate to the classroom.

#1: Nobody Seems to Care!

Teaching is always an adventure, and for beginners, navigating that road of potholes and speed bumps is an almost necessary part of the journey toward becoming an effective teacher. Finding ways to engage a roomful of hormonally charged teenagers hour after hour, day after day is not easy, and figuring out how to do it well can take years of practice, a point that David Berliner, the past president of the American Educational Research Association, makes clear.

> *Problems of discipline, effectiveness with both slow and rapid students, sustaining the interest of poorly motivated students, having a variety of materials that students liked to work with, and establishing a satisfactory set of requirements for the classroom were all judged as being accomplished in no less than five years for the majority of teachers.*[1]

Many of the teachers I interviewed made the same point. One of them remembers how disheartening her first months in the classroom turned out to be.

> *The kids didn't want what I had to give them. Here I was for them. I was their gift, I was going to work hard for them, I was going to give them what they wanted, what they needed, and they didn't want it. Nobody told me. What do you mean you*

don't want what I have to give you? What do you mean you are not going to eat this up? I am bending over backwards for you! Why would you want to throw spit wads at me? It was shocking. That was so disillusioning.

Another retired teacher also recalls how difficult his first weeks in the classroom proved to be.

What was really hard was when no matter what you did you still got the glazed eyes. That was frustrating to me. I know I really tried hard. Sometimes you know your class is not going to be all that exciting, but on days when you know you have really given it your best it is tough. This is the Federal Reserve and it is important, but it is hard to make it compelling. I tried really hard to make it mean something to the kids. Those can be long periods. At the end of some classes you just don't want to make much eye contact because you know it just didn't work.

And a longtime English teacher is mortified to remember his early years as a teacher: "I look back in horror at my first five years. It's almost like I want to contact my students and apologize." An especially pointed perspective on the difficult adjustments new teachers must make as they wrestle with the complexities of the classroom comes from this advice Margaret Metzger received early in her career, as quoted in her article "Maintaining a Life": "For the first three years of teaching, new teachers should pay the schools for the privilege of practicing on the children."[2]

The end result of that reality is that some choose to leave the classroom before they ever learn to master their craft, a fact that proves expensive both to the schools and to the students in them. If teachers consistently leave a school before gaining basic competence, that can only mean that the students in that building will be taught by a long line of newly minted teachers in the midst of on-the-job training. The financial impact of high teacher turnover is a problem as well; at the turn of the century, the Texas State Department of Education reported that the annual 15.5 percent turnover rate in that state cost Texas schools $329 million annually for recruitment and training.

#2: I Don't Know Where to Begin

While we might like to pretend that undergraduate education classes prepare prospective teachers well for the classroom, almost no one outside of the education departments at colleges throughout the country really believes that, because the challenges new teachers face are so daunting. No college training program can replicate the long hours of preparation and grading required of teachers at every stage of their career, and few twenty-two-year-olds understand the nuances of motivation and gamesmanship necessary to jump-start reluctant learners. While some student-teaching experiences are indeed able to open a new teacher's eyes to the challenges he or she will face, the truth is that too often the veteran teacher to whom the student teacher is assigned sees his or her presence as an opportunity to take the semester off and still get paid. Some supervising teachers *are* incredibly helpful (mine, for instance), spending hours with the novice teacher helping him to sort out whatever problems may arise. But some supervising teachers prefer to spend those hours by disappearing into the teachers' lounge to drink coffee while the student teacher struggles to survive. As a result, when new teachers finally enter the classroom, too many of them can fall back only on the handful of lessons they tried that actually worked during their student-teaching experience, their vaguely defined understanding of the art and science of teaching, and their memories of their favorite teachers in middle school or high school. And that's not enough. The average new teacher enters the classroom scared, ill-prepared, and filled with a few scattered theoretical ideas about teaching that may well collapse within six weeks—or even six hours—of the first day of school.

The result is that for too many young teachers, their first years in the classroom are an exercise in on-the-job training that leaves them filled with apprehension as they frantically rush to figure out how to stay ahead of the kids before they sniff out their teacher's anxiety and crush him or her as casually as a little boy squashing a spider beneath his Nikes. Knowing that they have to craft a credible lesson by Monday morning, new teachers do not have the luxury of spending a quiet Saturday afternoon in the hammock out back contemplating why they teach what they teach and what they are trying to accomplish through each lesson. They are slaves to the tyranny of tomorrow, so trapped by what has to get done that they have no time to determine why they are even doing it. In my experience, the pace of the school year overwhelms almost every new teacher.

Ryan Fuller encountered that shock when he moved from the space program into the classroom, as detailed in "Teaching Isn't Rocket Science: It's Harder."

> *As an engineer, I dealt with very complex design problems, but before I decided how to solve them, I had a chance to think, research, and reflect for hours, days, or even weeks. I also had many opportunities to consult colleagues for advice before making any decisions. As a teacher, I have seconds to decide how to solve several problems at once, for hours at a time, without any real break, and with no other adults in the room to support them. There are days of teaching that make a day in the office seem like a vacation.*
>
> *In teaching, a person can be extremely competent, work relentlessly, and still fail miserably. Especially in the first year or two on-the-job, success can seem impossible. For people who have been so successful up to that point in their lives—failure is a difficult thing to face, especially when that failure involves young people not being able to realize their full potential in life.[3]*

Many of the retired teachers I interviewed found it difficult to adapt to the demands of the classroom and balance them with their life outside of school.

> *The biggest adjustment for me was probably the time demands. Feeling like you were never done with papers, never done with planning. It was never a job I could just come home and say, "Family, I am all yours tonight." I was always feeling that tug that if I was being a good teacher this week then I was being a bad mom and vice versa. That was frustrating. I wanted to do both things well, and it was hard to.*

There was never enough time to do anything very well. You know the old **Horace's Compromise** *by Theodore Sizer? Everything was a compromise. Everything in life is a compromise, but in trying to do all of those different things I felt my life was so compromised.*

The sheer weight of responsibility comes as a shock to too many novice teachers, especially those who are unused to adult responsibilities; only those who have the gumption to cope in the expectation that things will change can hope to thrive. In their article "Why Do New Teachers Cry?" Thomas McCann and Larry Johannessen quote one young teacher they interviewed for their study.

I just thought, "I need to stick it out. It's probably going to be unpleasant for a while, but that's how I have to deal with it." . . . It wasn't like a passive endurance. During this whole time I was working my butt off trying as many different things as I could. I was racking my brain at night: "what can I do better tomorrow? Is it my lesson? Is it my behavior?" I was constantly thinking of things.[4]

#3: I Don't Get No Respect

The desire to stick it out is made more difficult by the lack of respect some teachers feel from the communities they serve. In a *Phi Delta Kappan* study designed to examine why so many teachers leave the profession early, Barbara Benham Tye and Lisa O'Brien quote one disgruntled ex-teacher dismayed by the low public esteem in which teachers are held.

It's obviously a no-status career when Laura Bush goes on TV to recruit the best and brightest to teaching for two years. The implication is that, after two years, these people will have done their public service and can now go on to real jobs that pay decent wages! The other implication is that currently the best and brightest don't choose teaching—that's insulting.[5]

One of the retired teachers also reflects upon the sting of disregard he has felt in some social situations.

> *I would run into people who would say, "Still teaching?" There was a sort of denigrating aspect to that question. That is an ego-centered thing, but the unspoken attitude was "You can't do any better than that?" That was always a bit of a dig.*

#4: These Kids Are Driving Me Crazy!

Another pothole that new teachers face is the battle with classroom management, a struggle that only intensifies the frustrations they experience. Because few twenty-two- or twenty-three-year-olds have any experience as a parent and are just starting to decipher how to be an adult, figuring out how to command respect is a major challenge for someone who only ten months before was storming the field to tear down the goalposts after a big game or drinking tequila shots at a sorority party. One of the great moments of truth for every young teacher comes during the first parent-teacher conferences of the year when the parents of a rowdy student ask the twenty-two-year-old "professional" for advice on how to get their child to cooperate. Whatever my answer to those parents may have been, I pray to God they did not follow it.

The lack of maturity, experience, and moxie proves fatal to many young teachers; nothing but stubborn pride kept me going my first year because I had no clue how to keep a classroom under control. The narrow age gap between new teachers and those they teach, especially for high school teachers, creates all kinds of problems. Knowing where to draw the lines of authority can be tricky, and being seen as an authority figure when the lunchroom ladies continually mistake a new teacher for a student only undermines his or her every effort to be taken seriously. One of the retired teachers puts it this way:

> *I think when I was really young it was a little harder to be an authority figure for them, especially given my personality, which is kind of warm. Those first few years when I was only a few years older than they were it was kind of hard to establish*

the difference. Here I am a warm person, but I cannot be your friend. It actually got a lot better when I was older and had children of my own. They saw me as an adult because of that.

Given their lack of experience in dealing with discipline issues, many teachers fall back on what they were subjected to as students to gain control, sometimes with results that in retrospect are embarrassing, disappointing, or worse. One veteran of more than thirty-five years of teaching recalls the ways he tried to discipline when he was starting out.

I grew up in an educational system in which control was everything. In high school it became pretty severe too. They would have you stand in the hallway holding dictionaries over your head if you messed up. I remember one of my teachers had a kid write a two-hundred-word essay on why a light bulb is brighter than he was. So that was what I was used to. I did some of those things. I taught in the neighborhood where I grew up. The kid down the street was going to be a seventh grader, so I drove him to school. . . . In the first week they had a recess, and he threw a mud chunk and hit a girl right in the eye. So I grabbed him and threw him against the wall. I had this kid up against the wall. How stupid was I? If I did that today, I'd be fired. But that was the aura I experienced in my education, so I thought that was the way it was supposed to work. I would like to go back and undo that.

#5: I'm in This by Myself!

The isolation inherent in many school cultures is another obstacle new teachers face in their efforts to adjust to the pace of the classroom. Though in the last decade or so, mentoring programs have become de rigueur in many school districts, the effectiveness of those programs depends upon the chemistry between the veteran teacher and the novice and their commitment to one another. Professional learning communities (PLCs) focused on common planning and shared data analysis also have gained a great deal of traction in recent years, but the lack of time devoted to them and the unwillingness of some teachers to engage in them in any meaningful way have made their implementation uneven. Every school culture is unique, and for every school in which mentoring programs and PLCs operate effectively, there are many others for whom those programs exist only on paper or not at all. As a result, teachers new to a building can find themselves alone and lost with no one to turn to for help. One forty-year veteran recalls his experience when he switched schools early in his career, trading a place where he felt supported and appreciated for one in which his department chair viewed him with suspicion because this new teacher had not yet proven himself. Alone, filled with regret and self-pity, he remembers the comfort he received when another teacher in the department stopped by to see him to offer a word of support.

> *One day I wasn't even having lunch because I was grading, and this wonderful teacher, Mrs. Madden, who had been there forever—had the soul of a poet, just a lovely lady—she knocked on the door. I was in tears because I was grading and thinking, "This is the dumbest thing; I shouldn't be here." She came in and said, "Are you ok?" I said, "I am really not." I guess I was mentored there for the next hour. She put her arm around me and said, "I have watched you. I have listened to you. You are a good teacher. I have some kids in creative writing who have you for class, kids that have a good sense of what is a good teacher. They think the world of you."*
>
> *I said, "I am not feeling that right now." I explained to her . . . I was overburdened and I came from a place where they loved me and I loved them. She helped me. She kept reminding me that I was a good teacher: "part of the problem was them [the other teachers in his department] and not you. I am also telling you that the guy who is department chair, if you do a good job, you will win him over eventually."*

Not every teacher is so lucky. Many first year teachers can only suffer in silence. Reluctant to expose their own vulnerability, they keep to themselves and toil endlessly and independently to master skills they have not yet acquired. A veteran teacher, later a principal, describes what it was like for him versus the way it should be.

Imagine yourself standing at the base of a mountain. You've never climbed a mountain before, you have never put crampons on your feet before and you're looking at it and there is nobody there to help you and you think, what am I going to do? And you start trying to go up that mountain. That, as opposed to someone coming alongside you saying, "Here, put these on your feet, put this belt around you. I am going to walk alongside you and do this together." That's a pretty graphic picture of teaching, with and without somebody to come alongside you who knows what you are doing and going through. In the early days nobody talked about mentorship. It was more like, "We are down the hall, come and talk to us." And they were nice people, but there was no formal plan to help. What do I do about attendance, how do I teach this lesson? I was on my own.

#6: You Mean I'm Supposed to Know What I'm Doing?

That isolation matters for many reasons, but the fact that few young teachers have a clearly defined philosophy of education or understanding of pedagogy only exacerbates the problem. Without mentors or administrators to guide them toward discovering what they believe about teaching or without a school-wide understanding of those issues that is widely embraced, a novice teacher is left to fumble toward an understanding of his or her basic philosophy. A standard assignment in many undergraduate education classes requires students to write their own personal philosophy of education. Because most prospective teachers have yet to think deeply about the task of teaching, their responses, however well-intentioned, are at best superficial and naïve. Mine were BS. I didn't know what I thought about teaching as a twenty-one-year-old. I had seen a few *great* teachers, a few more *good* teachers, a host of *mediocre* teachers, and a few *terrible* ones. So my philosophy was an amalgam of what I had seen from my favorite teachers flavored with snippets derived from the most popular educational thinkers of the day. When I actually stepped into my own classroom, I made it up as I went along, choosing texts and writing assessments based upon my best judgment on my good days and expedience on my worst. Young teachers are so busy balancing the demands of classroom management, planning lessons, grading papers, adapting to a new school culture, responding to parents, meeting with students at lunch or after school, and even coaching basketball or directing the school play that they do not have the "luxury" of developing a philosophy of pedagogy or curriculum. In *Educating for Life: Reflections on Christian Teaching and Learning*, Nicholas Wolterstorff points out the problem.

> *Incredible as it would surely seem to an outsider, should any discover it, teachers often have no conscious and reflective reason whatsoever for selecting one thing to teach rather than another. . . . Vast numbers of teachers just teach, teaching as they were taught, unreflectively exercising their ingrained habits, enslaved to custom, no more deciding what to teach and what to emphasize than the crow decides what song to sing.*[6]

One veteran teacher agrees that, based upon his own history, developing a meaningful philosophy is not a given for many teachers: "If you would have asked me ten years ago what my philosophy of education was, I would have just given you a bunch of words because I had never really sat down to think it through. I guess I had some implicit assumptions about what teaching should be, but I never looked at them in any systematic way."

#7: Testing, Testing, Testing

Even if teachers do have a clearly developed, coherent philosophy, external demands placed upon them may make the implementation of that philosophy impossible. The motivation behind the reforms instituted by No Child Left Behind and Common Core makes sense in a country in which the quality of education is so uneven, but the temptation to teach to the test or to measure the effectiveness of a classroom teacher by test results has a series of unintended consequences that can squelch a teacher's creativity and freedom. Particularly for schools whose accreditation is threatened, test day becomes the Super Bowl of the school year, a day in which the stakes are enormous, but when teachers and administrators have to beg kids to take these tests seriously, the potential for abuse is real. One retired teacher makes this very argument, pointing to his experience with his own niece, who was an honors student in the school in which he taught: "When it came time for the state test, Meaghan just filled in all of the bubbles randomly. If I couldn't even get a girl like her to take this seriously, how much weight can we really give to the results?"

Another teacher objects to the state tests precisely because they conflicted with his own philosophy and priorities as a teacher: "What the testing primarily does that I have a problem with is that it has put us in a prison of the way we evaluate. The more creative ways we can evaluate kids no longer exist." To another veteran teacher the entire premise of state-mandated tests is absurd.

> *Each time the state would come to us and say we're going to institute these new programs, they would try to convince us this was for better education. This isn't for better education. They are basically trying to force us to teach something that they want taught for some political reason. They would say, "No, we don't even want you to teach to the test." I would raise my hand and say, "Are you serious when you say that?" They would say, "Absolutely we are serious. As a matter of fact, we would consider that criminal."*
>
> *I'm not the brightest guy in the room, but I'm a distance coach [in track]. So this afternoon we go outside and I say to these people, "I'm going to get you ready for the state meet. You're milers, but let's go over and throw these shots, and then we are going to play a game of softball." They're going, "What?" And I'd say, "Exactly. If this test is important, then I should teach to the test, to teach them what you want them to know." They'd say, "We want to see if you're teaching them what we want them to know." I go, "This doesn't make any sense. That's my problem. There is no connection . . . If you are not teaching to the test, what's the point of even having a test?"*

So whether the issues are insufficient preparation, unrealistic expectations, excessive time demands, a lack of respect from the public, unruly students, professional isolation, an underdeveloped philosophical and pedagogical understanding of the craft of teaching, or the struggle to balance the demands of external tests versus the needs of the students, teachers new to the profession have a lot to learn. And the truth is, some teachers, even those in the classroom for years, continue to face those same obstacles.

As the Students See It

Since I taught seniors exclusively for the last dozen or so years of my career, I always assigned as their final essay a paper that asked them to reflect upon their experience in high school, detailing the good, the bad, and the ugly of their classes and their education in general as a way of learning from them what I might do better in my own classroom. One of the assignments the kids most seemed to enjoy was based upon the *Calvin and Hobbes* cartoon below.

CALVIN AND HOBBES © 1993 Patterson. Reprinted with permission of Universal Uclick. All rights reserved.

Using the cartoon as their model, I asked the students to create metaphors in which they described their experiences with their best and worst teachers. Outing their worst teachers by name was taboo, but the seniors could be brutal in describing the ordeal those teachers put them through. Here are some samples.

Some teachers turn us into robots because, instead of teaching, they fall into the habit of going through information and simply have us regurgitate it as if we were mindless machines. During these classes tests would simply consist of the notes that we had been expected to take in class put into multiple-choice questions. The test would require no comprehension, analysis, or investigation; it was simply a test of facts to see if we could memorize a worksheet. I would say it could not have helped anyone learn the material. These teachers would stand in front of class as if we were robots to be programmed. I would say that very few students in those classes probably understood what was being taught well enough to explain it in another context. It was not helpful information in the sense that the students could not take what they had learned and apply it to their lives.

I can vividly remember my most frustrating experience with a teacher. Walking into class every day was like being a bottle on an assembly line. I knew that the abnormally large amount of information that I would soon receive in a packet of notes would be flooded into my brain. Although I could not recall the contents ten minutes post-period, the teacher continually dumped loads of information in day after day as though I were a mere glass jar, able to retain it all without losing a single drop of knowledge. However, that is far from the truth. The unending amount of information was expected to be memorized verbatim for every test, and if every nugget of knowledge was not inscribed in an answer, points would be deducted. Making matters worse, she did not take time to explain the material clearly. Every day was PowerPoint after PowerPoint of cluttered notes; the information went in one ear and out the other yet was expected to be memorized by the following day.

In my worst classes I felt like I was sitting on a conveyor belt with a blank stare as a substance was poured into my head. I often felt as if meaningless information was being forced into my head as a teacher sat at the front of a classroom talking in a monotone about some subject that did not seem to pertain to my life in any way. In fact, often the teacher did not seem to even care about the information or the students' comprehension of it. It was as if the teacher considered teaching the material a boring and meaningless ritual. Any connection between the lesson plan and anything relevant was lost.

Reading these essays was painful. Though as a faculty, we created or attended workshop after workshop designed to spark innovative instruction, the students made it woefully clear that in too many instances we were missing the mark. Despite the leadership's efforts to insist that our teachers continue to grow, at least some of our faculty seemed stuck in the ways of the past, lecturing nonstop, insisting on rote memorization, and treating each class as an opportunity to pour a fire hose of information into their students' heads. Since I was the academic dean charged with teacher training and evaluation during this period, I regarded these responses as a personal failure, a reflection of my inability to persuade at least a few holdouts to take a hard look at what they were doing and why they were doing it.

What was most striking about the observations the students made was that in many cases the teachers they were describing had been teaching for years. Some had been part of our faculty for decades, and all of them had the credentials and degrees that suggested they knew their subject and they knew how to teach. But the inability of these veteran teachers to adapt to the needs of their students serves as a reminder of just how incredibly difficult it can be to teach well. The truth is, the potholes and speed bumps never go away. Though we expect brand new teachers to flounder in all of the ways listed above and more before finding their footing, the reality is that teaching is difficult for most people and can remain so for as long as they stay in the classroom; it can take years before young teachers reach a basic level of competence simply because the trials they face are so diverse, and veteran teachers face a different problem: they can become so locked into certain pedagogical approaches and beliefs that they become averse to change.

No teacher enters the classroom hoping to be mediocre. No teacher stands in front of a group of students on the first day in August and says, "This year I am going to bore them to death." But the words

H. L. Mencken wrote in the *Baltimore Evening Sun* nearly ninety years ago capture the unhappy truth of what a classroom can be at its worst.

> *The notion that schoolboys are generally content with their lot seems to me to be a sad delusion. They are, in the main, able to bear it, but they like it no more than a soldier enjoys life in a foxhole.... School days ... are the unhappiest in the whole span of human existence. They are full of dull, unintelligible tasks, new and unpleasant ordinances, brutal violations of common sense and common decency. It doesn't take a reasonably bright boy long to discover that most of what is rammed into him is nonsense, and that no one really cares very much whether he learns it or not.*[7]

It doesn't have to be that way. Great teachers spend their careers trying to make a liar out of Mencken.

Reflections

1. What are your biggest fears about teaching?
2. What are the qualities and practices of your worst teachers in middle or high school you want to avoid?
3. What are the qualities and practices of your best teachers in middle or high school you want to emulate?

Action Items

1. Who are the experienced educators you can turn to for counsel and advice? How are you going to create opportunities to meet with them regularly to talk through the issues confronting you?
2. How are you going to carve out time in your personal life to ensure you do not become so overcommitted to the job that you burn out?
3. If you could write a metaphor to describe the experience you would like the students in your class to have, what would that metaphor be?

Chapter Two
Defining What Really Matters

It is hard to make a liar out of Mencken, however, when beginning teachers have so little grasp of what they believe about teaching. One of the points raised in the previous chapter bears repeating because it is so critical to a teacher's long-term success: new teachers must establish their own identities as educators, a task made problematic by the difficulty of even knowing what questions to ask in preparing for their initial school year. Few rookie teachers have the luxury of walking into their first year with a clearly defined pedagogical philosophy in place; instead, they largely make it up as they go along, learning what works and what does not through trial and error. Focused on the next day's lesson, young teachers rarely can articulate why they do what they do since they are limited by their inexperience and driven by a curriculum they have not really thought through. For many, expedience drives their decision-making, not any fundamental beliefs that provide a philosophical framework for curricular planning. That is the point that Margaret Metzger makes in her *Phi Delta Kappan* article "Maintaining a Life."

> *It sounds easy enough to explain to students why they ought to do something. But brand new teachers often have no idea why they are doing something—beyond the fact that they have 180 days to fill. It takes a long time for teachers to develop the philosophical underpinnings for everything they do in the classroom.*[1]

Floundering to Find a Way

In an age in which professional learning communities and in-depth induction programs are becoming more common, Metzger's point may not be as universal as it once was, but the problem is still widespread and has been an ongoing concern for new teachers forever. Most teachers who began their career in the 1960s and 1970s faced incredible frustration, having no clear understanding of what they believed about teaching and little hands-on support from the administration. This was clearly articulated by a now retired career educator who left a corporate job at AT&T to report to his first day of faculty orientation in one of the most highly regarded districts in Missouri.

> *I felt about as out of place as I could possibly be. I sat down and started listening, and it was a lot of here's how we do this and here's how we do that, basically nuts and bolts. We went through about three days of that and they said, "Okay, school starts Monday." There was nothing about curriculum or philosophy or mentors or anything. It was kind of like, "If you need any help, let us know." And that was it. I thought, "What? I have never been around anything like this in all my life!" I had been through a graduate program and had an education degree, but I had been away from all of that for two and a half years. What did I know about teaching kids at that point? I had done my student teaching four years earlier, and now I had to walk in as if I knew what to do. There is nothing like, okay, all the eyes are on you . . . what do we do next?*

The decision of what to do next is often based upon nothing more than what new teachers themselves experienced when they were in middle school or high school. Few have any sense of what works and what does not. Few have any sense of what their goals for the year are or even should be. So they base their pedagogical approach on the way they were taught combined with whatever they learned in their undergraduate coursework. The results are often not pretty, as this former teacher remembers.

*The thing as I look back that I am more ashamed of than any-
thing is that I resorted to the way that I was taught. The education
process that I had to go through in school was that if you were
smart and worked hard you were rewarded, but if you screwed
around, boy, did they give you hell. They put you down, and the
message was, those kids are never going to make it. . . . When I
first started teaching, that's how I taught. You reward the good
kids, you laud the good kids and the bad kids, forget it—they need
to work harder. All those kinds of things were stupid.*

As I struggled to define the rationale behind what I was trying to
do in my classes early in my career, I turned to the wisdom of a wide
range of educational experts for inspiration. Like most young teachers, however, I found little help there since so many of these experts
seemed to define the purpose of education so differently. For instance,
here is a sampling of the smorgasbord of perspectives I encountered.

*Education either functions as an instrument which is used to
facilitate integration of the younger generation into the logic of
the present system and bring about conformity or it becomes the
practice of freedom, the means by which men and women deal
critically and creatively with reality and discover how to participate in the transformation of their world.[2]*

—Paulo Freire, **Pedagogy of the Oppressed**

*What is Summerhill like? Well, for one thing, lessons are
optional. Children can go to them or stay away from them—
for years if they want to. There is a timetable, but only for the
teachers.*

    *The children have classes usually according to their age, but
sometimes according to their interests. We have no new methods of teaching, because we do not consider that teaching itself
matters very much. Whether a school has or has not a special
method for teaching long division is of no significance, for long
division is of no importance except to those who want to learn
it. And the child who wants to learn long division will learn it no
matter how it is taught.[3]*

—A.S. Neill, **Summerhill**

I say the ends of education, the ends men should seek, are always and everywhere the same. They are absolute in the sense that they are not relative to time and place to individual differences and the variety of cultures. They are universal in the sense that they are invariable and without exception. . . . The ultimate end of education is happiness or a good human life, a life enriched by the possession of every kind of good, by the enjoyment of every type of satisfaction.[4]

—*Mortimer Adler,* The Paideia Proposal

So where is a young teacher to turn in trying to decide what he or she believes about education? The reality is that most teachers turn not to whatever educational gurus they may have been exposed to in an undergrad or graduate program but to their own experience or to the wisdom of their colleagues. As they flounder, they are forced to deal with their own inadequacies and try to figure out how to move forward.

What Are We Here For?

For me, the biggest obstacle to success in the classroom was not classroom management; it was not mastering the subject matter or even motivating the students. It was instead something so fundamental to the process of education that it is embarrassing to admit that it took me years to figure it out. In thinking about schooling, my focus was always on teaching, always on trying to understand how to master the tricks of the trade by incorporating the latest teaching strategy or instructional approach. My eyes were on my own performance, on my own technique, and in adopting that emphasis, I did my students a terrible disservice. Because my focus was on me and not them, I treated my students as bit players in a drama in which they should have been the stars. It was not until years into my career that at last, through the influence of other teachers in my building and educational thinkers of various stripes, the light dawned.

Teaching is not the issue. *Learning* is. For years—and it embarrasses me to say it—I thought my job was to present information clearly and creatively, and if my lessons met those criteria, I thought I had done my job. But teaching is an exchange of ideas, skills, and life lessons, and if the students do not participate in that exchange, then even the most imaginative lesson is a waste of time. Here is the bottom line: if the students do not learn, the teacher has missed the mark, no matter how noble his or her intentions or efforts. When students take a test, they are not graded on the teacher's sincerity in teaching with passion and preparation; instead they are graded on what they know, so if a teacher is unable to convey the information under review to students so that they understand it and can integrate it into their thinking, then learning has not taken place. The image at the left defines the problem perfectly. Teaching and learning ought to form a seamless partnership— you can't have one without the other. Except of course you can. Too many teachers adopt a David Farragut approach to the classroom: "Damn the torpedoes, full speed ahead!" Like Admiral Farragut hammering his fleet into Mobile Bay at all costs, too many teachers plunge on relentlessly, dashing through their material with more thought given to their timetable than to the ability of their students to grasp the material the teacher is so desperate to cover. But as Edward Fiske writes, "To truly reform American education, we must abandon the long-standing assumption that the central activity of education is teaching and reorient all policy making and activities around a new benchmark—student learning."[5] That's the bedrock on which all that we do rests.

In my job as academic dean, I sat in too many classes to count in which I saw students' eyes glaze over in total lack of interest while a teacher continued to plow through complex material oblivious to their boredom. I saw other students try frantically to get their teacher to explain some confusing concept only to have that teacher dismiss the students' question with a wave of the hand. One of the most unforgettable moments during my college days occurred in a course in the modern novel my junior year. After walking us through the syllabus on the first day of class, the professor pulled out his old, yellowed notes taken sometime during the Truman administration and began his introductory lecture. Thirty minutes in, another student raised his hand to ask a question. The teacher droned on, blind to the student's attempts to interrupt until that student said, "Sir, I have a question." The professor's response was classic: "I don't take questions in this class." This man was not a teacher. He was a dispenser of information, a man who saw his job as a one-sided process in which the students were largely irrelevant. For teachers like this, the textbook—or in his case his notes—drives the curriculum, and the need to cover the material supplants all other concerns.

It gets worse. To prevent any student from being buried under a flurry of tests and other deadlines, we instituted a test calendar at our school, one that required all teachers to submit their major test and due dates to an administrator to ensure no student would be asked to take more than two tests or turn in more than two major assignments on any given day. For the most part those test and assignment dates trickled in throughout the year, but a few teachers submitted their due dates for the entire year to the administrator in charge before school even began. That drove me crazy. It still does. How can a biology teacher know in August that his students will be ready to take the test on mitosis on February 24? What if the class misses three days because of a blizzard in January? What if this year's class is unusually advanced so that they speed through the material at a faster pace than anticipated? Or what if a history teacher plans a test on the civil rights movement for April 3 and a Trayvon Martin or Michael Brown incident sparks a national controversy concerning race relations at the end of March? Would it make any sense *at all* to slow the pace of the class and spend a few days talking about the implications of that event? One of the retired teachers shares that frustration.

> *There were teachers who planned out the whole next year in June. How could they do such a thing? If you lock into what you are doing in June, by the time you get to February, you are not going to have any clue about what they are doing. Did you know in June they were going to be ready for that test in February? You're going to beat it into a kid's head because you said you had to get there by February?*

Let's ask the obvious question: What matters more, the sanctity of a deadline or the welfare of the kids? One senior captures the essence of the problem in her year-end *Calvin and Hobbes* essay.

> *We are not empty bottles to be filled with facts and knowledge—we are human beings with creative minds eager to learn and explore our capabilities. Pouring in and out endless amounts of information sends our brains into overload. Learning a subject does not come from cramming facts down our throats and expecting homework to be completed each night. Rather, teachers should take a different approach, playing toward the strengths of the students and their capabilities.*

Idan Ravin understands that principle. An attorney-turned-basketball trainer, he is a teacher so gifted he attracts the elite of the NBA to hone their skills in special one-on-one sessions with him each off-season. Among his clientele are such superstars as Kobe Bryant, LeBron James, Chris Paul, Kevin Durant, and Stephen Curry. Rather than demanding that those he trains adapt to his methods, he says about his work, "It's not incumbent on them to understand me; it's up to me to understand them."[6]

That principle is essential to the traditional classroom as well. Teachers who blindly career ahead no matter the aptitude of their students are caught in the same trap I struggled with early in my career. They think—and I thought—that good teaching is all about them. But teachers who have figured it out know that good teaching is instead an interchange between teacher and student in which both have a part to play. Here is how one retired teacher describes the ebb and flow of the classroom between teacher and student.

> *Here is my job . . . my job is to make you smart. So your job is to ask questions until you get it. So if I say something to you and you don't get it, you ask a question, and I give you an answer. If you still don't get it, it's your job to say, "I still don't get it," even if that's all you can say—"I still don't get it." It's my job to figure it out. It's my argument that with weaker teachers, if you don't get it, they give you the same thing again, you still don't get it, and everybody gets frustrated, and they tell you to sit down*

and shut up. So I say to my students, "It's not your job just to be able to get it because I tell you. It's your job to keep asking me until you get it. It's my job to find different ways to tell you that answer until you get it or until you give up. Because if you say to me, 'Never mind I get it,' I'm done. But if you say to me 'I still don't get it,' . . . I am obligated to come back to you because that's my job. If you say to me, 'I don't get it,' I don't get to say to you, 'You're stupid' because that's not your job. Your job is to keep asking until you get it, and my job is to keep looking for ways to explain it until you do get it." Early on, I did what everybody else did. You asked me a question, I gave you an answer. If that answer didn't work for you, I'd let you go away. Later on I would say, "Does that make sense to you now?" I know to a certain extent how to interpret your response. "Yeah, I guess so" means no. Everything means no except "Yes, I get it." Everything means no except "I think what you are trying to say is da-da da-da." That's exactly what I'm saying.

So a fundamental lesson that every beginning teacher must learn is that the classroom is for the kids, not for the teacher. Teachers unwilling to enter into the interchange with students to do all they can to ensure that kids are actually learning miss the whole point of education. That is a hard lesson for young teachers to accept simply because of their inexperience, a point a longtime speech and debate teacher makes clear.

I think every beginning teacher—it is just the nature of the beast—you are defensive, you are self-conscious. You probably feel like it is a sign of weakness to admit any mistake or to do those do-overs, those mulligans. I got much better at being an evaluator of whether something worked or not. Then you have to make the judgment, OK, if we take an extra 90-minute block to go over what we did before, that means we have to give up something I had originally planned, but you are able to make those judgments. OK, we are not going to have time to go over semicolons or have to skip studying "Annabelle Lee" because we are going to take an extra two days to go over "The Cask of Amontillado." An experienced teacher is able to be more self-evaluative and make judgments about what is working and what isn't. When you begin you just don't have that field of experience to tell when things are working and when they are not working so well.

The need to slow down to reteach material students are clearly struggling with is something that good teachers should embrace but often do not. One of the retired teachers explains how he began to think about teaching well into his career.

> *I believe in going back if something didn't work. You'd say, "I thought we were going to do this on Wednesday, but we are going to go back to what we tried on Monday, and we are going to try it a different way. Something didn't work. Maybe it was me, maybe it was you, maybe it was a combination." You have to be willing to start over. You have to be willing to make adjustments. You have to be willing to say something didn't work. The worst teachers that I can think of were the ones who were the most dogmatic in terms of what they did or what they believed and just kept going.*

A hurdle new teachers must overcome in the absence of a core philosophy is the insecurity they typically feel due to their lack of mastery of the curriculum they have been assigned. Most beginning teachers enter the classroom on day one with only a rudimentary grasp of the information they have been asked to teach, so the first few years are a long, long sprint to stay far enough ahead of the kids to survive. Here is the experience of one high school history teacher: "The first five years I taught different subjects all the time, and though you can read ten books on World War I it doesn't mean you really understand it. You know enough to teach a high school class, but till you teach it you don't really know it." The temptation for a new teacher is to try to dazzle students with what he knows, a temptation I succumbed to too frequently in my early years. In preparing for my first ever lessons on *Macbeth*, I spent hours exploring the nuances of the Shakespearean theater and the Elizabethan worldview and then dumped everything I had just learned on my students in two overly detailed lectures. Perhaps 15 percent of the information I conveyed helped set a context for the play; the rest was simply showing off. Lacking the sophistication to know what mattered and what did not, I buried my students in an attempt to convince them I knew what I was talking about. I had the equation completely backward; the job of a teacher is not to convince the kids that he or she is smart—it is to convince the kids that they are, a point a retired English teacher makes clear.

> *One of the things I thought as I went through school myself was that teachers didn't try to make me feel smart. They tried to figure out what I didn't know often in a pretty public way. For the most part I didn't want to do that. For the most part I told kids at the beginning of the year, my job is to make you feel smart. It is like everything else. If you have confidence, you are going to do better. Now I didn't reach every student by a far margin, but there were kids you could see who did get it.*

The Conversation

A teacher who views his role in the classroom as convincing the kids that they are smart shifts the emphasis from himself to his students and recognizes that what matters is their progress, not a brain dump of way too much information. A few years ago I sat in an AP Art History class of a gifted but very young teacher who was racing through a lesson on Byzantine art. The students dutifully took notes as this energetic, driven young woman pointed out the distinctiveness of that genre with wit and clarity, highlighting the uniqueness of Byzantine style and subject matter. The teacher cared, she knew her stuff, and she clearly liked both teaching and kids. But in her rush to cover the material, she ignored a host of questions that might have captured the students' imaginations. She showed them, for instance, how the Byzantines' depiction of angels was unusual, but she never explained how the choices they made in painting them so distinctly reflected their view of the cosmos, of God, and of humanity. On a test the students could very probably distinguish between an angel painted in a Byzantine church from one painted in a Gothic cathedral, but could they have explained how each depiction reflected the artist's view of God and the church? Could they have explained how the way those artists drew the angels revealed their

worldview? In racing to cover the curriculum, this teacher was missing the point: Education is not just about conveying information—it is about stimulating curiosity, it is about creating opportunities for kids to ask questions they didn't even know to ask when they walked in the door on the first day of school. For this teacher, the driving force behind the curricular choices she made was the fact that her students would take the AP Art History test in May, and she wanted to ensure that she covered every chapter in the AP-recommended text so that the students would be prepared for the exam. However noble that goal may be, she was perhaps missing a larger point. As we debriefed her class the next day, I asked her to articulate her objectives for the course, a task she struggled to do. Together we brainstormed a number of possibilities:

- Students will score a four or five on the AP Art History exam given at the conclusion of the course.
- Students will answer these questions: What is art, how is it made, and how does it reflect the culture and time it represents?
- Students will both understand that behind every trend in art lies a worldview and be able to identify the worldview behind the different artistic genres and specific works of art discussed in the course.
- Students will appreciate the beauty of a wide range of art forms and be able to identify the distinctiveness of each.
- Students will learn that art is subject to a wide range of interpretations.

Undoubtedly those possibilities are incomplete and, to anyone with some degree of sophistication in the field of visual arts, might seem naïve, but each option defines the course differently and establishes priorities for instruction that would help shape a teacher's choices. Because she was brand new to AP art history and fairly new to teaching, this teacher had not taken the time to determine what she was after and why that objective was important. The guidelines from AP Central told her to cover a wide, wide range of genres, and she was determined to do it no matter what. But in doing so, she risked sacrificing the sense of wonder and curiosity that great art should evoke in her mad dash to get through the twenty-four chapters in her art history textbook. Here is the point: Unless a teacher has a clear sense of what she is after by seeking to steer her curriculum toward some overarching objective or objectives, then in all likelihood she will allow her curriculum to be driven by a series of unconscious choices that may not be best for the students or be true to what she believes about teaching. And too many young—and not so young—educators don't take the time to define what they hope to achieve because they feel so much pressure to conform to standards they are not even aware exist. Once she began to slow down, took the time to define the course according to her own and the school's objectives, and focused on what her students both needed to know and would be excited to discover, she began to thrive, and the students had the luxury of asking the kinds of questions that made art come alive to them. And her students did really well on the AP test too.

What this teacher had to learn is the importance of what I like to call The Conversation, an element of teaching that is as important as anything a teacher can do to awaken the students' interests and curiosity. A lot of what goes on in a classroom is a straightforward (and necessary) presentation of information. Kids need to know that the sinking of the *Lusitania* played a part in leading America into the Great War if they are going to understand why we got involved in 1917. They need to know that John Steinbeck wrote *The Grapes of Wrath* in response to the Okies' migration to California during the Dust Bowl years if they are going to understand the social tensions at work in that novel. They need to know that interest rates affect the ultimate purchase price of a car or house if they are going to be informed consumers. But if teachers stop there, they do their students a terrible disservice. Facts set a context, but they also open up opportunities for meaningful discussions of a whole host of issues that are relevant, challenging, and thought-provoking. If teachers do not have those conversations, they gut the ultimate value of what they teach, and they miss the sparks that can ignite so unexpectedly in the classroom. One of the mysteries of teaching that makes it so much fun is that teachers have so little idea of where a class discussion will go once it begins. Because every class is unique, The Conversation in third hour may take a direction radically

different from that taken during first hour. A student may ask a question or make a point that captures the imagination of the entire class and creates a whirlwind of ideas the teacher did not anticipate and may not be able to control. That is when magic intrudes, when the alchemy of interaction concocts a brew of inspiration that may resonate with a class for the rest of the year. A digression can be a waste of time, to be sure, but an unexpected question often means a student is thinking, and if a student is thinking, that means the teacher is doing his or her job. Here is how one of the seniors describes those serendipitous moments in his *Calvin and Hobbes* exit essay.

> *My favorite part of the year was when the teacher told us to put down our pens because we were going in a direction he didn't see coming. That's when we took trips into the Twilight Zone, a place of mystery and unpredictability. That's when learning became fun because no one saw it coming.*

I saw a missed opportunity for "mystery and unpredictability" when I observed a teacher present a lesson on President Truman's decision to drop the atomic bombs on Hiroshima and Nagasaki during a junior-level U.S. History class a few years ago. The teacher did an expert job of laying out Truman's rationale for his decision systematically and clearly, detailed the destruction the bombs caused, and talked about how the Japanese capitulated shortly thereafter. When a student raised her hand and asked if the teacher thought the decision to drop the bomb was morally correct, he said he did not have time to address that question because he wanted to wrap up the World War II unit quickly so the class could take a test on Tuesday. And then he moved on as if the student's question was unimportant. He did not talk about the controversy surrounding the decision then and now, did not ask the students to consider the evidence for and against dropping the bomb, did not ask the students to analyze the arguments that have been made in support of and in opposition to Truman's decision. The morality of the choice to drop the bomb has stirred disagreement for more than seventy years, but to the students in this teacher's class, it was as if the debate did not even exist. To ignore the controversy surrounding Truman's decision was to forfeit a chance to allow students to reflect, to engage, and to consider the consequences of what was literally a world-changing decision. It is important that students know that the United States developed and used an atomic bomb to end the war with Japan. But it is also important that students engage in The Conversation so that they can begin to form the moral compass that will help to define their adult beliefs. Had, for instance, the teacher divided the class into two groups, assigned one to read an article defending Truman's decision and the other to read an article attacking it, and then invited his students to engage in a debate that captured the critical ethical issues at play, his students would have had an opportunity to wrestle with the depths of the question and arrive at a personal perspective on what happened in August 1945. Unless teachers develop a philosophical approach to education that places a high value on such discussions, they risk becoming little more than human information dispensers.

Let's concede one point immediately: it is much easier to get to the heart of The Conversation in some disciplines than in others. It would be criminal to read plays such as *Death of a Salesman* or *Macbeth*, novels such as *To Kill a Mockingbird* or *All the King's Men*, or short stories such as "Babette's Feast" or "The Lottery" in an English class without delving into the moral quandaries those stories address. Events like the Dred Scott decision, the Army-McCarthy hearings, the Montgomery bus boycott, and the My Lai Massacre open the door to serious discussions in a history class. Debates over the controversies surrounding such issues as fracking, global warming, evolution, atomic energy, genetic engineering, and human cloning can play a part in making a science curriculum more than a study of the application of abstract concepts and formulas. While lower-level foreign language classes are restricted in their ability to engage in The Conversation because of the students' limitations in the target language, upper-level classes can certainly go there. At our school, for instance, students in French IV read Albert Camus's *The Stranger*, a novel that certainly offers plenty of meat for a teacher who wants to generate a serious discussion about critical life issues. Drama classes, music classes, and, as we have seen, visual arts classes all offer opportunities for conversations about issues other than technique. Even math classes present openings for big picture analysis, according to a former math teacher.

One of the problems with math is because math does have some practical applications—engineering and those types of things—people think that is its only purpose. People think you have to make everything practical and applicable. No, you don't. What we do as educators is we teach kids how to think. English teachers teach them how to think, whether it is reading a book or writing an essay. I teach them how to think by analyzing a problem. We teach them how to analyze, how to think, how to express their thoughts. They express their thoughts in one class by writing essays, in mine by writing out problems. You go down the social studies hallway, they read historical pieces and say this is what this side is saying and this is what that side is saying. We do the exact same thing. You do it in this context, and I do it in this context. We are both teaching kids to think.

The Three R's Are Not Enough

An approach to teaching that focuses on skill building and information dispensing is critical, of course. Students should know how to conjugate irregular *-ir* verbs in Spanish, read the periodic table of the elements, and locate Germany on a map. They should know how to balance an equation and a checkbook and how to distinguish a metaphor from a simile. But education should not—cannot—stop there. In interviewing teachers about their priorities over the years, the theme emerges again and again.

- From a high school English teacher: "It is essential that students learn to read and write in my class. It is equally essential that they grow as human beings."
- From a high school math teacher: "It is far more important to me that I influence my students' values than their ability to balance an equation."
- From a high school history teacher: "My goodness! I have the world at my doorstep in terms of ways for them to discover and understand more deeply what the human experience is and that there is nothing that they are going through that somebody else hasn't already gone through. All kinds of les-

sons that other people have learned are within their purview
to understand and to enrich and inform their lives . . . by what
we read, what we discuss, by what kinds of lessons we create."
- From a high school science teacher: "I think advances have
taken place in science such as cloning and genetics, genetic
engineering. To give some illustrations in biology, I am more
convinced than ever how important it is to have the students
who someday will be in these fields to have outstanding character and moral convictions in order to direct where these
avenues of research are going so they will be used for good
and not evil."

This desire to impact their students' inner lives reflects the almost
religious sensibility that many teachers seem to bring to the profession. John Van Dyk, while serving as an education professor at Dordt
College, routinely asked his students why they sought a career in education. Though they offered many reasons, he writes, "When I ask
all these folks to identify the one, single most compelling reason for
entering the teaching profession, I frequently hear . . . that they feel
called to be teachers."[7] Many of the teachers I interviewed said much
the same thing. For instance, here are the words of a woman who spent
her entire career in public education.

> *I really do believe in the idea of calling, that God wired us to do*
> *certain things. There are other things I could do, and probably*
> *do effectively, but I don't think I was called to do those things,*
> *so I would want to connect the whole idea to one of calling and*
> *that gifts are part of that.*

While others may not use such explicitly religious terminology to
describe their commitment to the classroom, many are nonetheless
driven by what Robert Gardner, in *On Trying to Teach*, describes as the
"furor" to teach as they bring what he regards as an "obsessive commitment" to the task.

> *Appoint an energetic man or woman to the teacher's job and in*
> *short order that teacher will regard as indispensable whatever*

he or she chooses to teach and whatever method by which he or she chooses to teach it. . . . The true teacher never rests.[8]

Teachers with that kind of drive—whether they would view their profession as a calling or not—see their duty to their students as serious business and are willing to invest their lives imparting not only knowledge and skills but in addressing matters of the heart as well.

In his book *The Road to Character,* *New York Times* columnist David Brooks reflects on the tension we feel in a society that celebrates achievement but sometimes ignores the importance of a rich inner life. Here is how he defines the problem.

> *Recently I've been thinking about the difference between the résumé virtues and the eulogy virtues. The résumé virtues are the ones you list on your résumé, the skills that you bring to the job market and that contribute to external success. The eulogy virtues are deeper. They're the virtues that get talked about at your funeral, the ones that exist at the core of your being; whether you are kind, brave, honest or faithful; what kind of relationships you formed.*
>
> *Most of us would say that the eulogy virtues are more important than the résumé virtues, but I confess that for long stretches of my life I've spent more time thinking about the latter than the former. Our education system is certainly oriented around the résumé virtues more than the eulogy ones.*[9]

Great educators recognize the importance of teaching to both virtues. Information matters enormously in a society that must have competent accountants and computer programmers, physical therapists, and dental hygienists. No one wants to be victimized by an electrician who does not know how to wire a light fixture or by a bank teller who does not know how to add. But great teachers know that their job is about more than being a conduit of information; they must seek to instill in their students a love for learning, a passion for ideas, and a fascination with the wonder of the world. And they must help students to see that their life will be defined by more than a six-figure salary and a degree from a prestigious school. Teaching is a profession for idealists, and to be successful at it is to cast a higher vision for students than the cynics in society would ever advocate. It is about passing the torch to the next generation so that they may make contributions to a world unimaginable today. Here is how one twenty-seven-year veteran of teaching explains her attitude.

> *Leo Buscaglia, the Love Doctor, said in the intro to one of his books that his idea of a teacher was always a bridge across a chasm. And he said basically kids are on one side, and you want to get them across to the other. You throw yourself across the chasm, and the kids cross over you. They're fine, you fall into the chasm and you're done. That's not a bad description of a teacher's role. It's not all about me. It's all about the kids.*

Only when educators take the time to think through why they teach what they teach can they begin to view their work as a bridge across a chasm that students must learn to cross. So much of what is of value in the classroom arises spontaneously, and teachers who are insensitive to those moments when a student asks a critical question or makes an offhand comment that may steer the discussion into unknown territory may miss the opportunity to shift the axis of a student's thinking. Since those moments arise so unexpectedly, a teacher never knows when what he or she does will make a real difference. A retired English teacher describes the process this way.

> *I do feel like I made a difference in kids' lives. In one way it is so mundane. They come into your class, they go through the vocabulary words, they write essays. It is so mundane, but on the other hand it is so significant. It all adds up. Those little discussions we had, those little comments a classmate makes that open someone's eyes to a new way of thinking. It all adds up, and I do feel like for a lot of kids I don't feel like it is me that did it but creating an environment in the classroom so they could do it for each other. Giving them the ideas that help them think, help them crystalize who they want to be. That's what I gave them. It's not that I did that, but I gave them that environment of a place to think, a place to grow, a place to experiment and learn about the world. That's what changed them. That's what helped*

take them from where they were at the beginning to where they were at the end. That's rewarding—that I gave them the gift of the year that helped them get from A to B.

Even when teachers foster that environment, even when they consciously seek to create a climate in which The Conversation takes place, they may never know how the lessons learned take root in their students' lives. While we may think we are teaching kids how to write an effective topic sentence or how to play the trombone, what the students remember may be far different, a point one former teacher makes in the following statement:

I have come to the conclusion that I have little idea of what I have really taught the students in my classes in a given year. When students come back to visit a year or five years or ten years after their graduation to talk about their experiences in my class, it always seems that they didn't learn what I thought I was teaching. Instead, they learned all kinds of lessons I didn't know I was teaching at all.

That's the mystery of The Conversation. That's why The Conversation matters. We *are* to teach skills, we *are* to impart information, but we are also to create an environment in which kids are free to explore ideas we can never anticipate or control. When we do that, we allow teenagers to form their own view of the world, shape their own values, create their own understanding of the critical issues of the day. We allow them to work out their eulogy virtues as well as their résumé virtues under the guidance of someone invested in their academic and personal growth. Only teachers who share that focus, who have thought through why they do what they do, can structure their curriculum and their classrooms to inspire kids to investigate what they really believe. Stephen Kaufmann, a professor at Covenant College, argues that the best education challenges kids to ask hard questions in search of making a difference in the world because they have been engaged in wrestling with meaningful discussions and have seen the gap between what the world is and what it could be. This is his idea of what education should be about.

For a couple of minutes I would have you consider that instead of producing competent, well-adjusted students, maybe our schools should be producing competent, maladjusted students. By maladjusted students I don't mean those who are psychologically unhinged, but rather those who have developed a keen sense of the discrepancy between the world as it is and the world as it ought to be. You see, maladjusted kids would find the hedonism, relativism, and racism of our day to be profoundly unsettling. Maladjusted kids would dream about and begin to work for a world characterized by justice, compassion, and moral integrity.[10]

Turning out maladjusted students may not be everyone's goal. Some, in fact, might strongly object to it. What Kaufmann suggests, though, is a way of looking at education that is purposeful, intentional, and consciously chosen. A teacher who embraces Kaufmann's vision—or one similarly philosophical in nature—will choose readings, create assessments, and encourage class discussions that will ask students to measure their core beliefs against society's expectations. That kind of deliberate planning defines the flow of an entire course and establishes priorities in ways that a textbook cannot.

Given the demands of planning lessons, writing tests, and grading papers, young teachers may argue they do not have the time to invest in the heavy mental lifting that leads to a clear understanding of what they believe about teaching and that delineates what they do in the classroom. To avoid that work, however, means that teachers allow others to define their philosophy of education for them, a decision Plato would regard with disdain: "Wise men speak because they have something to say; fools because they have to say something." A teacher's curricular choices—indeed, his or her career—should not be measured by the need to "say something." They, and it, should instead be defined by a system of consciously chosen priorities and practices designed to help the students flourish to the best of their ability. Surely the ultimate goal of education cannot be limited to covering the material in a textbook or striving to ensure that every student gets a five on an AP exam. Educators whose vision is limited to such ends miss much of the fun of teaching and deprive their students of the opportunity to wrestle with the ideas and experiences that may most engage their minds and may most impact their lives. All of those undergraduate education professors who ask their students to write a philosophy of education are on to something. The problem is, of course, that few juniors in college know enough to write a philosophy that makes any real sense. But any teacher a few years in has experienced enough failure and has taken enough body blows to see the value of taking the time to figure out what matters and what does not. If experience is the best teacher, then young teachers should take the time to turn that experience into a foundation for the rest of their career.

Not every teacher's vision of what the classroom experience should be is driven by the same degree of philosophical focus as is Kaufmann's. The late Jim Shapleigh, for instance, spent sixty years of his life in education as a classroom teacher, a counselor, a principal, and then, in retirement, as a volunteer tutor in the school district in which he had served. Early in his career, he wrote a personal philosophy of education, one he used as a touchstone for the next fifty years and later passed on to his son, a man who taught high school math for thirty-one years. Reprinted below, it serves as a testament to one man's vision of what he believed about education, a vision that deals far more with relationships than with the kinds of outcomes Kaufmann envisioned.

The Teacher Code

> I WILL . . . like and respect my students.
> BECAUSE . . . I recognize they are special and unique individuals.
> I WILL . . . sincerely want my students to succeed.
> BECAUSE . . . if they know this they are more likely to be motivated.
> I WILL . . . have and share a sense of humor.
> BECAUSE . . . kids love a good laugh and will be more at ease and I will be more human.
> I WILL . . . be fair.
> BECAUSE . . . if I am not, they will resent my efforts and resist learning.

I WILL . . . be patient.

BECAUSE . . . young people are sometimes prone to making mistakes in judgment and response.

I WILL . . . expect frustrations.

BECAUSE . . . disappointments are par for the course. I should not panic or lose control.

I WILL . . . initiate reconciliation.

BECAUSE . . . in a student-teacher conflict the student may not know how to mend the fences.

I WILL . . . avoid, when possible, public reprimands.

BECAUSE . . . no student enjoys being taken to task in front of classmates.

I WILL . . . smile often.

BECAUSE . . . the responses from a pleasant exchange and smile are positive and rewarding.

I WILL . . . be prepared.

BECAUSE . . . knowing the subject and being organized will give my students confidence in my skills.

I WILL . . . be honest.

BECAUSE . . . if I make a mistake, students will respect me more if I admit it truthfully.

Those words may not match what another teacher would write or believe. They may not touch upon every point that someone else might deem important. But they suggest the power of one man's commitment to understand what he valued so that he could walk into the classroom each day with a clear vision of who he was, why he taught, and what he hoped to accomplish. He was a man who "had something to say" because he took the time to determine how he viewed his duty to his students and how he would treat them. Kaufmann's goal is to teach toward an expected outcome. Shapleigh's goal was to concentrate on his relationships with his students as a springboard to their success. Though far different in focus, both approaches lay a foundation that helps define each teacher's core beliefs about education. Both men took the time to think through *why* they teach and in so doing established the framework for the units, the lessons, and the decisions that followed. My father used to say as I was growing up, "If you don't know where you are going, you'll get there every time." Teachers who do not take the time to articulate what they believe and why they believe it will get somewhere by June, but it may not be where they hoped to go when the semester began or where their students need to be. Think of the advantage the students of the teacher quoted below had simply because she knew exactly what she wanted to accomplish each day and why she wanted to accomplish it.

> *I told my students on day one, if you want to know why I do something in the classroom, ask me. I have a reason. And it is a reason based upon what I believe about you, and it is based upon what I believe about your brainpower and your capabilities and what I believe about the teaching and learning contract. It will be right there for you because I do that first. Guaranteed.*

Every student needs teachers who approach the classroom with such clarity. The demands of daily lesson planning and paper grading may make it difficult, but figuring out where teachers want to go and why that destination matters is far more important than most teachers can ever imagine the moment they set foot in the classroom on day one of their career.

Reflections

1. What will you do when your students fail to learn at the pace you anticipate?
2. What does The Conversation look like in your subject?
3. Have you identified those controversial issues within your curriculum that will provide fodder for The Conversation and structured your curriculum to allow time for those discussions?
4. What résumé virtues will students gain by being in your class? What eulogy virtues can you encourage?
5. How can you balance the desire to take time for The Conversation with the demand that you keep pace with the standards designed by your school or district?

Action Items

1. Have you identified your core beliefs about why your class really matters? Can you write a one-sentence statement defining why this class and curriculum are important and what you hope to achieve in the time you spend with the students this semester/school year?

2. Can you explain why each unit you teach matters in preparing your students for their next year in school, for their next stage in education, and for life beyond the classroom?

3. Does allowing time for The Conversation mean you must sacrifice some of your content? Prioritize those concepts that are absolutely vital for your students to master or information that they must have so that you know what can be sacrificed and what cannot if time becomes tight.

Chapter Three
Defining What to Teach

In his autobiography, Ben Franklin relates the story of a conference that took place in Lancaster, Pennsylvania, in 1744 between agents of the government of Virginia and representatives of the Iroquois Confederacy. At the conclusion of the conference, Virginia's commissioners offered the Native Americans an opportunity to send six of their finest young men to college in Williamsburg to be schooled in all of the "Learning of the White People." After taking a day to consider the offer, the Indians' spokesman responded with the following words.

> *We are convinc'd . . . that you mean to do us Good by your Proposal, and we thank you heartily. But you who are wise must know, that different Nations have different Conceptions of Things, and you will therefore not take it amiss if our Ideas of this kind of Education happen not to be the same with yours. We have had some Experience of it: Several of our young People were formerly brought up at the Colleges of the Northern Provinces; they were instructed in all your Sciences; but when they came back to us they were bad Runners ignorant of every means of living in the Woods, unable to bear either Cold or Hunger, knew neither how to build a Cabin, take a Deer or kill an Enemy, spoke our Language imperfectly, were therefore neither fit for Hunters, Warriors, or Counselors, they were totally good for nothing. We are however not the less oblig'd by your kind Offer tho' we decline accepting it; and to show our grateful Sense of it, if the Gentlemen of Virginia will send us a Dozen of their Sons, we will take great Care of their Education, instruct them in all we know, and make Men of them.*[1]

Both the white commissioners and the Native American leaders in Franklin's account believed in the value of education. Both agreed that the purpose of education was to train young men—and it was young men only in those days—in the expertise and in the ethos of their respective cultures so that they could function well within them. But because their view of what was necessary to thrive in each society was so divergent, neither side could even begin to agree on what essential information and skills should comprise the curriculum needed to prepare a young man for his role in the community. Though their basic beliefs about the purpose of education were identical, their views of what should be taught could not have been more different.

So even the task of defining one's philosophy of education is not enough. Teachers must also take the next step of deciding what competencies, concepts, ideas, and information can most effectively move their students toward the goals that best support that philosophy. In short, teachers must define what really matters and what does not, and must align those decisions with their core beliefs about education. Though the ability of individual teachers to design curriculum independently of district, state, and even national standards is more limited today than in the past, as teachers grow in their competence and confidence, part of their responsibility is to ensure that their students can both meet those external standards and master those concepts and ideas that the teacher and his department consider most vital to a student's long-term success.

How Much Can We Really Do?

All teachers struggle to limit the scope of their curriculum. As an English teacher, I had a seemingly infinite number of stories, poems, and novels from which to choose, and to pretend that we had covered the field in a year-long British literature class was an exercise in absurdity. Choosing six or so novels, a play or two, and a representative sampling of poems and short stories hardly did justice to the depth of the literature that has poured out of the British Isles beginning with the days of *Beowulf*. The problem is even more complex in science and history. Each year brings new scientific discoveries and adds to the pages of history, and unless teachers are driven by a clearly defined sense of why they do what they do, can they even begin to winnow the amount of information available to them to a manageable sample? When I was in high school in the late 1960s, our study of American history ended in 1945 on the deck of the battleship *Missouri*. The minute the Japanese signed the treaty ending World War II, history stopped, and the events of the Eisenhower and Kennedy years were effectively banished from the curriculum. When I moved into my role as academic dean in 2002 and began to observe other teachers regularly, I was alarmed to see that nothing had changed at our school. U.S. history was frozen in Tokyo Bay, and the birth of Israel, the Cuban missile crisis, the civil rights movement, Vietnam, Watergate, the Iran hostage crisis, and the Gulf War had apparently never occurred. Mikhail Gorbachev, Ayatollah Khomeini, Malcolm X, Martin Luther King Jr., Osama bin Laden, Lyndon Johnson, Bill Clinton, Ronald Reagan? Irrelevant. Somehow our history department deemed the tariff debates of the nineteenth century more important than the events and people that were actually impacting the lives of the students every day. Until teachers ask some fundamental questions—like what really matters—they will be ruled by precedent or by the textbook, and as the base of knowledge expands in every discipline, students will increasingly be poorly served by their teacher's failure to take a hard look at her curriculum. In *A Time to Learn*, George Wood asks a critical question.

> *As we expand what we know in virtually every field, textbooks merely get longer, with no attempt made to separate the wheat from the chaff. The clearest examples of this in my own work have occurred in our most recent searches for new science and history books. After hearing publishers' representatives glowingly describe how their books have been updated to include all the newest discoveries and latest events of historical significance, I would ask just one question: What was taken out to make room for more material?*[2]

Wood recognizes one of the primary tensions that exists in education today: the push so many teachers feel to cover the material in their textbooks. The classic battle between depth and breadth will only become more intense as the base of knowledge expands and teachers feel the time squeeze of a nine-month school year. That is why teachers must be purposeful in determining what must be taught versus what is covered in their textbook. Students *need* to know certain information. Other information is merely *nice* to know. The best teachers know the difference and therefore make conscious choices to distinguish between the two based upon their educational philosophy and the needs of their students. This is how Robyn Jackson says it in *Never Work Harder Than Your Students*.

> *Rather than trying to cover as much as possible, master teachers are strategic about what they teach and how they teach it. They understand that it is the quality, not the quantity, of learning experiences that matter. Master teachers first determine what students absolutely need to know and how well they need to know it before deciding on what learning activities they will use to help students master the objectives. . . .*
>
> *When we are in coverage mode, we focus students' attention on completing rather than understanding. The idea seems to be that if we have covered it, the students must understand it. Grant Wiggins and Jay McTighe call this "teaching by mentioning it."[3]*

Again, the priority must be that the students learn, not that the teacher simply presents a blizzard of information. Though the pressure to cover all the material in a textbook seems irresistible to some teachers and to some districts, those schools that work hard to align their curriculum both horizontally and vertically can counter some of that pressure. If the Spanish II teacher knows that the kids in Spanish I were able to master only the content through chapter 17 and never got to chapter 20, then she knows where to begin next fall with that group of students. But for that adjustment to be made, communication within a department is critical, and in schools in which teachers act as independent agents free to teach what they prefer based upon their own predetermined timetable, that kind of communication will rarely occur. Only when schools embrace the idea that learning trumps coverage can a faculty embrace a more student-centered attitude: if the kids have not learned at a pace required to get through every chapter, then the teachers will adjust accordingly. Speaking at a Mid-Continent

Research for Education and Learning (MCREL) conference in 1999, Robert Marzano said, "Everything I know about good content means you've got to slow down, you've got to slow down, you've got to slow down. If you believe in racing through the material, I've got nothing to say to you."[4] That perspective only makes sense when teachers agree on why they are in the classroom in the first place. Grant Wiggins and Jay McTighe offer this reminder in the article "Put Understanding First."

> *The mission of high school is not to cover content, but rather to help learners become thoughtful about, and productive with, content. It's not to help students get good at school, but rather to prepare them for the world beyond school—to enable to them to apply what they have learned to issues and problems they will face in the future.*[5]

Defining the *Why*

It is easy to lose sight of that perspective given the pace of the school year, but teachers who focus on student learning first must confront what will and will not be covered by June. The necessary work of determining what should be taught is often ignored by teachers too inexperienced to make that decision themselves, but it is an essential part of the maturation of an educator. The immediate objection, of course, is that such a decision places too much power in the hands of a teacher, and certainly teachers who work in a system in which professional learning communities and departments function well and district or administrative oversight is in touch with the students' needs are best guided by those collaborative systems. But no one is better placed to weigh the needs of a specific group of students than the teacher, and it is important that teachers consider the needs of the actual kids sitting in an actual classroom alongside of the demands of external standards to decide what to teach and when to teach it. One teacher with whom I worked for many years kept a sign on her desk that read "What's best for Johnny?" Each curricular choice she made was in terms of that question. She recognized that tailoring the texts she assigned and the assessments she gave to the twenty-two students sitting in her class in a given period served them better than choosing books she liked or bowing slavishly to a curriculum that had been mandated to her from above. Teachers who bring that kind of thinking to their department can help to create a climate in which the needs of the students are paramount, and the entire department seeks to understand how it can adhere to the standards required of the state or district while still serving the students well by giving them meaningful work that will both challenge and intrigue them.

Early in my career I encountered the absurdity that followed a teacher who allowed her own whims to determine the curriculum rather than deciding what to teach based upon what the students needed. Hired to teach a course in American literature, I walked into my (previously her) classroom and saw shelves full of the novels she had selected for that class, including Charles Dickens's *A Tale of Two Cities*. Whatever my limitations as a teacher may have been at the time, I at least knew that Dickens's connections to American literature were suspect at best and asked our department chair to explain how Dickens managed to sneak onto the reading list. He explained that the teacher I had replaced was a Dickens fanatic and believed that every student should be exposed to his writing at every opportunity. Whatever Dickens's merits, he did not make the cut as I designed my curriculum that year.

I saw the same principle at work in observing a teacher introduce a unit in poetry many years later. An amateur poet himself and a man who had concentrated on the study of poetry in his graduate work, he spent the first two days of that unit defining the types of poetry he expected his students to be able to identify on a test. So he explained terms like *villanelle, rondeau,* and *terza rima*, identifying rhyme schemes and metric patterns to the exclusion of practically all else. I served as an English teacher for more than forty years. I like poetry. I even read it for pleasure. But I have no idea what any of those terms mean. Though they may be of value for a graduate student in poetry, they are of little interest or significance to a fifteen-year-old high school sophomore. Trying to get students to embrace the beauty and power of poetry is difficult enough without reducing its study to arcane terminology more typically found in higher academia. This teacher's interests trumped his students' needs, and their body language told me all I needed to know about their reluctance to buy in to his agenda.

It took years for one of the retired teachers with whom I spoke to begin to look at his curriculum through the eyes of his students and ask how he could put their interests above his own. He now looks back on his early years teaching world history with a sense of embarrassment and recalls his initial resentment of his students' indifference to his priorities: "I thought 'How can they not want to know who won all three of the Punic Wars?' I look at my notes from back then and think 'Wow!' You've got to start somewhere, but 'Wow!' It is amazing that kids are so compliant that they'll put up with this." Later he began to frame his curriculum with specific students in mind.

> *I had a girl, Ellen Kent [name changed], who was a pleasant, personable kid who couldn't care less about history. But she showed up and she was compliant, and I would say to myself, "If I can't justify why Ellen Kent should care about this, I shouldn't do it." It was . . . the realization over time that they are not evil because they are not into social studies. How arrogant was I as a young teacher?*

Two former teachers agree that over time they learned to think of their students first in designing their units and individual lessons. Here is how a former English teacher describes the way her curricular choices evolved.

> *I remember thinking, "I like this stuff, so I can probably make the kids like it too. Plus, these books are classics, so kids need to know it." Later I began to think along the lines of what questions really matter to the kids, what do I want to talk about with the kids to help them wrestle with their worldview, and what material can I give them to help facilitate those discussions?*

The second puts it this way: "I can't fall to the temptation of teaching what I like best or what I have been doing for the past five years. The question I have to ask is, how do I find material that will achieve my curricular goals, will challenge the kids, will interest the kids, and will help them to become the absolute best they can be?" In saying that she sought material that would both challenge her students and "help them to become the absolute best they can be," this teacher puts her finger on a crucial issue all teachers must consider in designing their curriculum. Choosing texts and creating projects of interest to students is not enough; the choices teachers make should be geared toward propelling those kids toward academic maturity and developing a sense of wonder about the subject under review and the world beyond.

Those goals become at least possible when teachers engage students in meaningful work that connects with their lives so that their curiosity is stimulated and their knowledge base expands. But too much that goes on in the classroom runs exactly counter to that end. ESL specialist Berty Segal's lesson on Martian math presents a classic example of the deadening effect of the worst of bad teaching.

> *In this chapter, we will be concerned with a study of the Pexlomb. A pexlomb is defined as any Zox with pictanamerals which flotate the Zox into five berta Zubs where each Zub is supramatilate to the Rosery of the Ord. For example, consider the Zox defined by 3 berta Ooz. It is obvious that any pictanameral which is Blat must necessarily be Cort to the Ord. This follows from our knowledge of the relationship of a dentrex to its voom. However, if the Ord is partivasimous, then the Zox must be Zubious. Thus, if we Kizate the dox pictanameral, our Zox will be flotated into 5 berta Zubs. But remember, each Zub must be supramatilated to the Rosery of the Ord.*[6]

Assigned a five-question worksheet as homework to decipher this lesson, most students could come to class the next day ready to explain that "if the Ord is partivasimous, then the Zox must be Zubious." But the meaning of those terms would remain a blur, and the reason for even discussing them would be wholly unclear. The unhappy reality is that though Segal's example may be amusing, the point she makes is deadly serious: too much of education follows this pattern exactly. Teachers present information with little context or connection to students' lives, ask them to memorize a series of unfamiliar terms with little or no relevance to any adolescent, offer no rationale to explain why any of this matters, and are shocked when the students react with utter disinterest. My high school biology class mirrored this approach.

Though my teacher was a nice enough man, he repeatedly asked us to memorize a catalogue of information while making no effort to tell us how anything he said connected to anything outside of the textbook. I studied the terms, took the tests, and walked away from the class with no interest in or knowledge of biology. His class was a perfect example of what Albert Einstein had in mind when he said, "It's a miracle that curiosity survives formal education."

The mistake that too many teachers make is that they never ask the simple question, "Why am I doing this?" If we only teach disparate information without showing kids how it can be used or without establishing any context for that information, then why should those facts ever matter to a sixteen-year-old? If we merely ask students to memorize facts or plug in formulas with no real understanding of what purpose those facts or formulas serve, then we are essentially inviting students to treat their education like a game of intellectual bulimia, encouraging them to gorge themselves on all that lies before them and then purge themselves of it once the test is over.

My son Jeff was an indifferent student throughout middle school and high school, the kind of teenager who dutifully did what he was asked by his teachers but with little enthusiasm or interest. Since I taught in the school he attended, I knew far more of his business than most parents are privy to, and because of that, he rarely asked for help with any of his homework or test preparation. To my shock, he approached me at home the night before a test in freshman English, asking me to help him learn the differences between various types of clauses and phrases he would be asked to identify on the test. As I looked over what he was expected to know and quizzed him on the various options, I was struck by how irrelevant this must have seemed to Jeff and wondered why he was being asked to memorize information that would have helped only someone trying to diagram a sentence. Both because I was his English teacher's mentor and was curious about why my son had been asked to memorize such arcane distinctions, a few days later I approached that teacher, a young man in his first year who was bright, committed to learning how to teach, and great with the kids, to ask him why learning to distinguish between all of those phrases and clauses mattered. His answer was simple: this information was in the textbook. At least to me, that was not exactly a highly defensible rationale. Textbooks are a helpful resource, to be sure, but allowing a text to dictate what should be taught seems at least questionable. When I asked Jeff's teacher what purpose learning to identify the different types of phrases and clauses served, his answer was that he was trying to encourage his students to develop the discipline of using sentence variety in their writing. I believe in the merits of sentence variety. I believe in mixing things up so that a person's writing style does not become predictable or boring. But never—*never*—have I sat at my computer thinking, "I haven't begun a sentence with an infinitive phrase for three paragraphs. It's time to throw one in there right *now!*" If this young teacher was trying to encourage sentence variety, there were better ways to do so. Due to his inexperience, he had not thought through what he was really trying to achieve and had succumbed to the temptation to blindly follow a textbook that was not all that helpful in getting the students to master the objective he was after.

In *Extraordinary Teachers: The Essence of Excellent Teaching*, Fred Stephenson argues that great teachers win the learning battle by establishing the "why" before the "what." Their objective, he says, is "to create a more relaxed, open-minded classroom atmosphere and to make learning enjoyable rather than punishing."[7] By clearly establishing for themselves why they do what they do and by explaining to students why they teach what they teach, teachers have a greater chance of getting buy-in from the kids who otherwise might be mystified by what they are being asked to study.

The importance of establishing the purpose behind what students do especially matters when the material a teacher presents is appallingly, yet unavoidably, dry. Though I promised my students each year on the first day of school that I would do everything I could to avoid assigning them busy work, a few times a year we faced certain inescapably low-interest topics they needed to know yet cared little about. For instance, when it came time to write a research paper, I had to explain how to format a Works Cited page and give them the proper form for in-text citations. Short of hiring clowns and jugglers to go over the details while Beyoncé boogied in the background, the information was coma inducing, so my go-to approach was this: I acknowledged that what we were about to do was hopelessly dull, tried to make the presentation as painless as possible by giving them handouts that reinforced everything I said, and promised that tomorrow would be better. And then I had to make sure it really was. Essentially what I learned to do was to think like a teenager and ask myself how to make each lesson connect to the world of an adolescent if at all possible; if not, I told them upfront that today would be a grind and relied upon their goodwill and trust in my promise that, as Scarlett O'Hara so often proclaimed, tomorrow would be another day. Leveling with the kids when they are in for a tough period can buy a teacher time as long as the students know that what they are forced to endure actually leads to a payoff. That's the point that Margaret Metzger makes in "Maintaining a Life."

> *High school teaching requires energy and drama. But flash without substance is mere gimmickry. Therefore, teach what is important. Don't claim that something is important if it isn't. Be truthful with students about whether you are required to teach material or whether that material will lead to more interesting ideas.*[8]

Learning to think with the mind of a teenager is one of the adaptations a now retired teacher embraced as he tried to figure out how to reach his students.

> *I had to learn how to put myself in the position of a student and remember what it was like sitting in that chair. Because you came out of school when you were force-fed, and all of a sudden all the eyes are on you, and you are in charge. You know what you want to do, and you know what you want that lesson to be, but to turn it around and say, "What does this look like from the other side of the desk?" matters. That was the one thing that I learned pretty early on that I tried to do. As I honed that skill, it served not only me, but it served my students as well. It is not all about disseminating information. It is not all about what I want to accomplish. It's about how do I get this information across to you and how do you receive it?*

Information or Analysis?

The ability to see what goes on in the classroom through the eyes of an adolescent matters for another reason as well. Though educational leaders have for years preached the importance of a student-centered approach to teaching, many of the speakers, articles, and books on that topic seem to focus on the *activities* that go on in a classroom rather than the *outcomes* those activities are geared to produce. So while experts extol the use of project-based learning, Socratic seminars, and cooperative learning as tools to empower students to deal with critical issues and key ideas on their own, they sometimes miss the larger point—that any classroom activity ought to be aimed at helping students acquire skills, sharpen their worldview, and engage their curiosity so that they can explore their life's passions with integrity and zeal. Emphasizing *how* to learn matters more than dictating *what* students must learn. Challenging students to read with comprehension, to think analytically, to consider alternative points of view, to dissect a problem from different angles, to write clearly, and to dream creatively are components of a sound education designed to help students leave their formal education behind in hot pursuit of whatever may delight them going forward.

Although most teachers receive occasional notes from students grateful for their experience in class, few notes strike as deeply at the heart of what education should be as does this email sent to a teacher the summer after the student graduated from high school.

> *You will never believe this. Well, you might, but I would be surprised. Your class totally altered the way I think, the way I write, and the way I learn. I just thought you'd be interested to know that the papers we wrote in your class were the most helpful and interesting assignments I have ever been given. . . . My previous learning was as a rat in a cage, to use an analogy. Rats do what they need to do to get the cheese. I was taught what to think. I was great at spitting out what I thought my teacher's [sic] wanted to hear, but I didn't have a clue how to think for myself. The scariest part is that didn't seem to be a problem. I got the grades but still wasn't interested in what I was learning.*

Through your assignments I found my motivation. I spent the entirety of the summer trying to make up for lost time. I read more books for fun than I've ever read in my life. I also learned how to ask questions and dispute things. I was always the kind of person who would agree with whatever I read. I never had a problem accepting what I heard. . . . The questions you asked got me thinking about what I was supposed to be getting out of my time in high school. I realized that I hadn't learned to think but had been doing what was necessary to get the cheese (to return to the analogy). . . . I wanted you to know how your assignments took my eyes off the specific details and helped me see the big picture of learning.

This student would have left her senior year having gained certain competencies to be sure, but it was not until her final year in high school that she began to understand that an education is not only about amassing skills that may prove helpful in a career, but is about embracing the value of learning itself. In a sense, an educator should follow the advice one of the retired teachers received from his principal early in his career: "'You are a scholarly role model. You are showing them an alternative way to be.' I kept that to the end and I thought that was a helpful perspective." Teachers are to serve as role models for the power of curiosity and the wonder of big ideas, for the sense that there is always more to know, more to uncover, more to explore. In "Maintaining a Life," Margaret Metzger encapsulates this way of looking at education.

Emphasize how to learn rather than what to learn. Students may never need to know a particular fact, but they will always need to know how to learn. Teach students how to read with genuine comprehension, how to shape an idea, how to master difficult material, how to use writing to clarify their thinking.[9]

Information will always matter, but in a world in which far more information than we can ever master is available with a few clicks of a mouse, passing on the zest for learning and the curiosity to keep asking questions matters far more. Good teachers know that the greatest gifts they can give to their students are a desire to know more and the tools to do exactly that. One of the retired history teachers said he wanted to give his students "a new pair of glasses, a way to see the world that they had never seen before. . . . [He] started off with this idea: 'We have definite and indefinite articles in our language and I am going to show you *a* way of seeing the world differently otherwise than you would have.' That's a goal that at the end of the year they have some tools to see the world differently." Helping students to write better or paint better or speak French better or balance an equation better is valuable. Helping them to see the world differently can change their lives forever. Teachers who think about education in this way need to consider carefully what they teach and why they teach it because the best education has little to do with whether a teacher prefers to lecture or lead a discussion and even less to do with a student's GPA or class rank. In *Let Your Life Speak: Listening for the Voice of Vocation*, Parker Palmer identifies the problem adolescents face in the classroom: "As young people, we are surrounded by expectations that may have little to do with who we really are, expectations held by people who are not trying to discern our selfhood but to fit us into slots."[10] Good teachers help students master skills and absorb information the teacher deems important. Great teachers help students find their own slot by helping them to discover who they are and giving them the tools to become the person they have been created to be.

Reflections

1. What is the worst-case scenario if you cut 15 percent of your curriculum to enable your students to really learn the material in your subject? What would be gained by slowing down?
2. How much are the curricular choices you make based upon each of the following criteria?

    - State standards?
    - District standards?
    - Personal preference?
    - Test prep?
    - Students' needs?

3. What steps can you take to ensure that you both meet the requirements defined by state and district standards and still appeal to your students' curiosity and questions?
4. What are the questions that matter most to your students concerning tomorrow's lesson?

Action Items

1. Can you identify the *Why?* in each of your classes? In each of your units? In each of your lessons?
2. What should you cut out of your curriculum so that you focus on what kids *need* to know?
3. Which of the standards you are expected to meet provide opportunities to engage your students' curiosity and interests?

Chapter Four
Defining How to Teach

In the wake of America's entry into World War I in 1917, the rush of young teachers to enlist or to seek employment in the defense industry was dramatic. Schools in this country faced such a shortage of qualified teachers that University of Illinois professor Charles Elmer Holley wrote, "This dearth is so great that, although every device has been employed to fill the vacancies in our schools, many schools have been closed because no one could be found to do the work." He added a stark warning: "Since the average teacher usually puts in only a few years of service before marrying or taking up some more gainful or congenial occupation, it can be seen that our schools are in crisis."[1]

In the article, "Ignorance of U.S. History Shown by College Freshmen," published in the *New York Times* on April 4, 1943, Benjamin Fine wrote, "College Freshmen throughout the nation reveal a striking ignorance of even the most elementary aspects of United States history and know almost nothing about many important phases of this country's growth and development,"[2] implying that with the country fighting for its life against the Axis powers, such ignorance posed a threat to Americans' sense of national identity.

The public's uneasiness about the quality of education only accelerated in the 1950s. In an article published in its October 16, 1950, issue, *Life* magazine released the results of a Roper poll on the state of schools in America that revealed that only one-third of adults were satisfied with the effectiveness of their local school. After the Soviet Union launched Sputnik, the first satellite to orbit the earth, the federal government appropriated the equivalent of $8.1 billion in today's dollars through the National Defense Education Act (1958) to address the fear that students in American schools were falling behind Russian students in their preparation in science and math.

So the sense that a crisis looms in American education is nothing new. Although reports that the math and reading scores of students in this country continue to lag behind the leaders internationally are certainly alarming in today's globally competitive world, and the ongoing achievement gap is too, the truth is that no golden age of American education ever existed in which all students had access to quality schools and learned at an impressive level. After all, it was not until 1940 that even half of all eighteen-year-olds actually graduated from high school. Further, whether it has been through the publication of the Coleman Report during Lyndon Johnson's administration, the creation of the Department of Education during the Jimmy Carter years, the release of the study "A Nation at Risk" during Ronald Reagan's first term, the passage of the No Child Left Behind initiative under George W. Bush, or the rise of the Common Core standards during Barack Obama's time in office, the federal government has been seeking the magical blend of carrots and sticks to best address the perceived and actual inadequacies of American schools for decades. But when Theodore Sizer, the former head of Harvard's Graduate School of Education, was asked by a reporter to name one reform of the previous fifteen years that had dramatically affected the quality of education in this country, he responded, "I don't think there is one."[3]

Sizer's comment resonates with the many retired teachers who witnessed a wide range of experimental innovations come and go throughout their career. As one of them said, "There were trends in teaching training in our school—Madelyn Hunter, Ted Sizer—that the district would lock onto that would be the thing at the moment, so teachers would have training in that. Two years later it would be something new." Tired of hearing the drumbeat of talk about the revolutionary changes in play for twenty-first-century education as the millennium approached, the standard retort for one of the teachers in our building became "The qualities of a good twenty-first-century teacher are not much different from those of a good fourteenth-century teacher," a point of view echoed in the title of Evan Keliher's critique of school reform published in *Education Week*, "If It Wasn't

Around in the Middle Ages, It's a Fad!"[4] Perspectives like these reflect the sense of fatigue many teachers experience when faced with successive waves of school improvement plans.

Is Teaching a Science or an Art?

But such fatigue does not give teachers an excuse to tune out the reams of research that help to clarify what works and what does not in the classroom, or to stick to outmoded modes of instruction that are of limited value. It is true that all teachers bring their own style to the classroom, but that style does not give teachers carte blanche to discount research that may point to better ways of promoting student achievement. Whatever their preferred approach, teachers cannot ignore the science of teaching, the results of the years of study that indicate which strategies and tactics most enhance student learning. Instead, teachers who continue to grow throughout their career are those who seek to blend their personal gifts with the findings of those academics who offer their own contributions to the conversation. As Leonard Pellicer argues in "Effective Teaching: Science or Magic?," "Those of us who have a concern with improving the quality of instruction make a serious mistake . . . when we spend our time praying for teachers rather than applying the available technology to improving the craft of teaching."[5] Linda Darling-Hammond concurs, as her observations published in *Educational Researcher* make clear.

> *Reviews of several hundred studies contradict the longstanding myth that "anyone can teach" and that "teachers are born and not made." Teacher education, as it turns out, matters a great deal. The most successful teachers not only have adequate preparation in their subject matter, they have also studied the art and science of teaching.[6]*

Rather than simply relying on their own preferences or convenience to define their methodology, teachers have an obligation to stay abreast of the findings of those researchers who take a comprehensive look at secondary education. That being said, Robert Marzano, one of the leading educational academics in the country, offers this caveat in *The Art and Science of Teaching*: "It is certainly true that research provides us with guidance as to the nature of effective teaching, and yet I strongly believe that there is not (nor will there ever be) a formula for effective teaching."[7] The truth is that no matter what the latest pedagogical innovation may be, real advances in education depend on the quality and commitment of the men and women in the classroom, many of whom are skeptical of the ever-changing appeals for reform sounding from on high since veteran teachers have seen a long parade of such reforms come and go over the course of their careers. And while the voices of those engaged in exploring innovative educational approaches are helpful in clarifying what does and does not work, Mike Schmoker makes an important point in *Focus* in citing the research of Jeffrey Pfeffer and Robert Sutton: "It is critical that schools learn the lesson that 'best practice' in effective organizations is rarely *new* practice. On the contrary, the most effective actions are 'well-known practices with the extra dimension that they are reinforced and carried out reliably.'"[8] And, Schmoker adds, "We will never master or implement what is most important for kids if we continue to pursue multiple new initiatives before we implement our highest-priority strategies and structures."[9] So while there is no magic bullet, no specific pedagogical panacea to cure the ills of American education, certain principles and practices do increase the likelihood that teachers can effect real change in students' performance in school. The problem is that too many schools become so wrapped up in the ongoing demands of the academic year that they do not even recognize that what they are doing has only limited effectiveness.

It is difficult to admit this, but for years the school in which I taught for the bulk of my career did little to systematically examine and define the fundamental principles that would govern "our highest-priority strategies and structures." Though our school was filled with many excellent teachers who cared deeply about education and the kids, and though we had a principal who was a committed, inspiring leader, we were essentially free to shape our own curriculum, develop our own pedagogical style and philosophy, and collaborate only when it suited us to do so. Many of us read deeply in the literature about teaching, but we never collectively codified what we believed or determined how our practice reflected those beliefs, and if anyone embraced the latest research in education, that was nothing more than a happy accident. It was not until we were challenged to develop a philosophy of curriculum and pedagogy following our formal accreditation review twenty years ago that we began to do the necessary—but to that point overlooked—work of systematically determining our core beliefs about schooling to ensure that our practices aligned with our understanding of what we valued and with what really works. A dozen of us spent several weeks over two summers hashing out the fundamental philosophies that defined our vision of educational excellence, reading a host of research from a bevy of educational leaders to guide our discussions and spending hours challenging each other's thinking.

In "Teaching and the Balancing of Round Stones," Gerald Duffy makes the case that teaching should be a reflection of a teacher's personal values and so wrote questions like "Why am I in teaching? What do I want to accomplish as a teacher? What indispensable message do I want to communicate to my students? What do I want my students to ultimately become?" to guide teachers to uncover a sense of their identity as educators. The ultimate goal, Duffy argues, is for individual teachers to develop a clear understanding of how their priorities and values in the classroom affect their practice.

> *Gradually . . . the teachers began to think hard about what really counted for them as educators and to articulate their personal intentions and values. As they did, they began to understand that decisions about the daily dilemmas of teaching had to be consistent with their values for what they wanted children to become. Slowly they developed the "Sense of alignment" . . . crucial for balancing round stones; that is, their values as individuals came into line with their professional intentions for children and schooling. Gradually these thoughts grew into "vision statements"—their very personal descriptions of what they cared about as educators.*[10]

Our task was much more difficult. We had to consider questions like Duffy's for our faculty as a whole as an initial step in reaching a "sense of alignment" concerning what we believed about education. One of the issues we struggled with was just how prescriptive we should be in trying to define what good teaching looks like. Some on our committee argued that a great teacher is an artist, one who, like all artists, understands the technical elements and technique of the craft but adds his or her own dash of imagination to the classroom. Arguing that one-size-fits-all innovations would meet resistance from those who might be asked to adapt a style or technique incompatible with their personal beliefs about education, some feared that we would rob our best teachers of their freedom to let it flow if we tied their hands too tightly. They pointed to those researchers who argue that teaching is more art than science for support. For instance, Donald Thomas in "Education's Seven Deadly Myths" makes a case for the creative side of education: "Teaching is an art. One becomes a good teacher in the same way one becomes a good actor, a good poet, a good musician, a good painter. One develops a unique style, a personalized method, a way of teaching that cannot be mass-produced or even replicated."[11]

That belief was buttressed when Larry Cuban, who conducted a comprehensive review of the evolution of teaching practices over a hundred-year period, identified those approaches with the most staying power, but concluded in *How Teachers Taught: Constancy and Change in American Classrooms, 1890–1990* that in the end such findings have their limits.

> *They do not capture the artistry of teachers who can individualize instruction with the nod of a head, the wink of an eye, and a friendly arm around the shoulder, or the abundant exchanges between students and teachers that produce a classroom culture complete with traditions to be honored and roles to be played.*[12]

So we had to wrestle with the fear that defining good teaching too narrowly would rob our faculty of their unique gifts and would thus be counterproductive. In the end, we agreed that the best teachers are artists *and* scientists, men and women who know what they believe about teaching but listen to the voices of those who can bring the wisdom of research to the classroom. In our view, Shawn Glynn, in "The Psychology of Teaching," seems to capture the right mix in his assessment of good teaching.

It is my belief that teaching is both an art and a science. The artistic side taps creativity and motivation, whereas the scientific side taps technical knowledge and methods. My metaphor for good teaching, the kind of teaching to which I aspire, is that it is a craft—an honorable, ancient craft, like that of a potter. A potter must be a good technician to create functional pottery, but there is much more to the craft than this. There's the artistry, or the potential for artistry, in the creation. That's what distinguishes expertise, be one a potter or a teacher. A teacher should integrate the art and science of teaching, resulting in an effective and unique style.[13]

The Steps of Learning

Once past the hurdle of identifying our basic beliefs about teaching, we concurred that though we did not want to dictate our school's philosophy so narrowly that it would rob teachers of their creativity, we could embrace certain core beliefs and principles about schooling that would unite us in a common understanding of what great teaching looks like. We did not want to create a straitjacket that would limit our teachers' freedom to bring their own flair to the classroom, but we did want to provide a blueprint to help teachers build structures and practices in the classroom that reflected our consensus concerning what great teaching actually is.

Our starting place for that consensus became an understanding of what it means to actually *learn*. For years I believed the ultimate measure of my students' progress was reflected in their grades since I never seriously considered any other option. Like many of my colleagues, I failed to see that a grade was a deeply flawed gauge of the student's learning since it rewarded those who were good test takers or could parrot the party line but did not indicate who had really wrestled with the issues we were discussing or who had internalized the importance of the content. As we analyzed the research to reach a common understanding of what learning really means, we encountered the same perspective again and again, a viewpoint that Grant Wiggins and Jay McTighe outlined concisely in "Put Understanding First" many years later.

Learning for understanding requires that curriculum and instruction address three different but interrelated academic goals: Helping students . . .
   1. Acquire important information and skill
   2. Make meaning of that content
   3. Effectively transfer their learning to new situations both within school and beyond it.[14]

Others make the same point using different terminology. For Robert Marzano, the three steps in the learning process are to acquire and integrate knowledge, extend and refine knowledge, and use knowledge meaningfully.[15] For *New York Times* columnist David Brooks in "Schools for Wisdom," the three steps are basic factual acquisition, pattern formation, and mental reformation.[16] And for Donovan Graham, a former education professor at Covenant College, the steps of learning are the *what*, the *so what*, and the *now what*.[17] Though the words they use to identify the three steps of learning vary, the message from each of these thinkers is the same. For learning to become deeply embedded in a student's mind and heart, it must include more than a simple transfer of information from teacher to student. That concept became the starting place for our common understanding of what good teaching looks like.

The *What*

In *Make It Stick*, Peter Brown, Henry Roediger, and Mark McDaniel support the idea that learning means more than simply demonstrating the ability to pass a test or reel off a set of facts. Instead, they write, it means "acquiring the knowledge and skills and having them readily available from memory so you can make sense of future problems and opportunities,"[18] a formula that fits nicely with the multitiered view of education outlined by Wiggins, McTighe, Marzano, Brooks, and Graham. For learning to take root, students must undertake the first step of the learning process by mastering a certain set of skills or internalizing a broad range of knowledge. In every discipline, students must become proficient in a basic body of information to serve as a foundation for further discovery and mastery in that area. Algebra students must understand the distributive property; chemistry students must understand how to read the periodic table of the elements; history students must understand what caused the Cold War; German students must be able to distinguish between *umsteigen* and *einsteigen*; band students must understand how to read music; English students must understand how to write a solid concluding paragraph. Basic vocabulary and ideas, dates, important people, skills, techniques, formulas, theorems, and principles are all the foundational building blocks for becoming an expert in any field. To put it simply, teachers must give students the context and concepts necessary to serve as the starting point for mastery of any discipline. Borrowing Graham's terminology simply because it was the easiest to remember, our study committee decided to call this step the *what* of the learning process. Before students can begin to deal with the complexities in any field, we agreed, they have to become conversant in the basic body of knowledge inherent to that discipline. Brown, Roediger, and McDaniel say that this stage in the learning process is the vital first phase in gaining the expertise necessary to flourish in any subject.

> *Mastery in any field . . . is a gradual accretion of knowledge, conceptual understanding, judgment and skill. These are the fruits of variety in the practice of new skills and of striving, reflection and mental rehearsal. Memorizing facts is like stocking a construction site with the supplies to put up a house. Building the house requires not only knowledge of countless different fittings and materials but conceptual understanding too. . . . Mastery requires both the possession of ready knowledge and the conceptual understanding of how to use it.*[19]

Though only a starting point for education, the *what* is a necessary first step. Without it, students will flounder to make sense of the issues they are asked to confront and to perform the basic tasks central to mastering any discipline. Although some might argue that the real value of an education lies in teaching students to analyze difficult problems, process complex information, and make inferences from the material in front of them, until students gain a basic competency in and information about any field, their ability to accomplish any of those undertakings will be severely limited. Here is how the authors of *Make It Stick* reflect upon that reality.

> *Pitting the learning of basic knowledge against the development of creative thinking is a false choice. Both need to be cultivated. The stronger one's knowledge about the subject at hand, the more nuanced one's creativity can be in addressing a new problem. Just as knowledge amounts to little without the exercise of ingenuity and imagination, creativity absent a sturdy foundation of knowledge builds a shaky house.[20]*

The *So What*

While it is important for students to understand basic terminology and concepts central to any discipline, it is also important that they take the second step in the learning process: they must understand the relevance of what they study. Teachers whose instruction provides only factual data are missing the mark; instead, teachers must build upon that base of essential information by demonstrating to students that the facts under review in some way connect to their lives. So students need to know not just that World War I lasted from 1914 to 1918 and a few random facts about Wilson's Fourteen Points; they need to know that promises made in the wake of that war have led directly and indirectly to many of the unresolved problems in the Middle East today that touch students' lives every time they fill up their car with a tank of gas or they turn on the evening news to hear about ISIS's latest atrocity. They need to know not just that *The Great Gatsby* is a book about a doomed love affair but is also a critique of the emptiness of materialism and the vanity of pursuing ill-chosen dreams, a critique as timely in the age of the Kardashians as it was in 1925. And they need to know that learning how to chemically alter the structure of molecules can impact American foreign policy as we transform one compound (corn) into another (ethanol) in an effort to end our dependence on Middle Eastern oil and address alternative energy sources. So a foundation of essential information is important, but the relevance of that information, what we called the *so what*, counts as well if teachers are to convince students that what they are studying really matters.

The *Now What*

The final stage of the learning process—what we called the *now what*—is the process by which students take the knowledge they have wrestled with in the classroom and actually make it part of their lives both in and beyond academia. To some degree, the *now what* happens naturally in any course. All classes, for instance, require students to make use of new information as it accrues throughout the school year; knowledge in any class builds upon itself so that ideas and skills that are at first theoretical become part of a student's way of thinking and doing as the year unfolds, as the *what* of the first semester becomes the *now what* of the second as students put to use what they have learned. Math students use the problem-solving skills learned in September to address new types of problems in February; foreign language students use the vocabulary and grammar of Spanish I to succeed in Spanish II; band students use their practice in playing scales acquired in the first weeks of the semester to play increasingly sophisticated pieces as the year unfolds. At its most basic level, then, the *now what* simply means that students understand and utilize the logical, deliberate sequence of information and skills necessary to become proficient in a specific discipline.

Ideally, however, the *now what* lessons of any education extend beyond commencement. The graduate who travels to Paris and uses her French skills to buy a train ticket to Lyon demonstrates that she has integrated her four years in French class into her daily life. The graduate who works in magazine design after serving on the yearbook staff, the accountant who accurately audits a company's books after taking accounting, the CEO who writes crisply and concisely in communicating a business plan to the board of directors after completing a writing curriculum, and the sculptor who designs a well-crafted piece of artwork for the city park after acing an art class are all making use of the competencies they developed in school. Part of a teacher's job is to teach students the skills they will need to thrive as they move into adulthood and pursue a career or a personal interest.

But seeking to integrate knowledge into students' lives means more than preparing them for a vocation or an avocation. For teachers whose classes are more theoretical than skill-based, measuring the *now what* can be difficult. Ethics teachers who challenge their students to explore the implications of issues like abortion or racism or war, or English teachers who ask their students to write about serious social issues can't really measure if those classroom practices have any lasting influence on the students. The truth is that the most meaningful *now what* moments may be invisible. A teacher's casual comment or well-timed question may resonate in a student's heart in ways that a teacher never knows. Really, the task of the teacher is to create experiences, craft assignments, and ask tough questions that will force students to examine their beliefs, look beyond their narrow world, recoil in outrage, or delight in a sense of wonder. Teachers need to help students wrestle with serious concerns and see their connection to their lives, but in the end the process of learning is complete only when students take what they have learned and make it part of who they are, what they believe, and how they conduct their lives at work, at home, and in the community. That is when the *now what* becomes real in the world beyond middle or high school. The goal, according to a now retired teacher, is this: "We have to lay a knowledge base necessary to engage in this discipline, but we are inviting you to join us on the journey, a journey we hope ends in delight and flourishing."

Learning That Matters

The *what*, the *so what*, and the *now what* became the foundation for our view of learning and provided the genesis for the sense of alignment that Duffy encourages all educators to seek. Of course we tried to make our instruction relevant long before our faculty committee began to meet that summer, and of course we had always believed our students' education would impact their lives far beyond the day of graduation, but explicitly defining these goals helped our teachers to speak with a common vocabulary and teach with a common purpose. And as our teachers began to embrace the importance of including the elements of the *so what* and *now what* in their daily lessons and assessments, they started to see their students think more deeply than ever before.

Katharina Wilson's argument "In Praise of Holistic Teaching" reflects the emerging recognition within our staff of the importance of making the *now what* an essential part of the curriculum.

> *If we can teach young people skills such as creative, reflective and analytical thinking and values such as empathy and the worth of diversity; if we can give them confidence and passion to continue learning and not fear the new, then we will have accomplished a feat far more important than the imparting of facts.*[21]

Based upon her perspective, teaching that involves the *now what* enables students to access critical ideas, skills, and information when needed, engenders within them the ability to think both creatively and empathetically, and inculcates within them a hunger to keep learning. One of the retired teachers defines his overarching focus on the *now what* this way: "Teach students how to learn. Stuff doesn't matter as much as how to learn the stuff. So reading with comprehension, asking questions, learning to research, how to persevere through difficult material, how to engage with an author. That's what I tried to do." That definition may not touch on every aspect of learning that really matters, but at least that teacher had a decent grasp of the sense that his job was not simply to present facts to a captive audience. Or as Tony Wagner in his *Education Week* article "Secondary School Change: Challenge and the Three R's of Reinvention" writes, ... "Increasingly all students must learn to reason, communicate, problem-solve, and work collaboratively. The skills now needed for work, college, and active, informed citizenship are essentially the same, but they are often not the skills being taught in many so-called college preparatory curricula."[22] So the best kind of teaching is geared to a three-step process that gives students the opportunity to lay a foundation of skills and information that enables them to wrestle with key ideas, ask serious questions, and draw meaningful conclusions in concert with others.

Neal Postman, the author of *Technopoly*, extends that point by maintaining that schools have an obligation to help students formulate their own worldview.

Perhaps the most important contribution schools can make to the education of our youth is to give them a sense of purpose, meaning and interconnectedness in what they learn. Modern secular education is failing not because it doesn't teach who Ginger Rogers, Norman Mailer, and a thousand other people are but because it has no moral, social, or intellectual center. There is no set of ideas or attitudes that permeates all parts of the curriculum. The curriculum is not, in fact, a course of study at all but a meaningless hodgepodge of subjects. It does not even put forward a clear vision of what constitutes an educated person, unless it is a person who possesses "skills." In other words, a technocrat's ideal—a person with no commitment and no point of view but with plenty of marketable skills. [23]

Sut Jhally, a professor at the University of Massachusetts, offers a one-sentence prescription for education that reflects Postman's thinking: "One of education's goals ought to be to get the fish to think about the water." [24] In other words, the job of a teacher is to create experiences that will cause students to reevaluate their unexamined assumptions and consider them anew. Garry Trudeau's *Doonesbury* cartoon captures the danger of an uncritical acceptance of information unfiltered by a thoughtful analysis of its relevance and truth. Part of a teacher's job is to help students develop the ability to think for themselves, not just mindlessly succumb to the point of view of other people. To help them do that, the best teachers seek to build upon what students already know while pointing out any added layers of complications they may have never considered. As one of the retired teachers said, "What's that line? Not to know one's history is to always remain a boy, so you are going to have a more mature understanding of how we got where we are. It's the invitation into complexity and paradoxes, the part of history you really don't see in middle school or grade school. Those were my macro goals." Another former history teacher sought to use the students' existing knowledge base as a point of connection to help them see the depth and importance of the issues they were studying.

I was not a disseminator of information. I was a creator of experiences. If I could make the unknown real to them, they could

say, "Wow! . . ." They'd get sucked in. They couldn't help them-
selves because they had something to hang it on. . . . I think it is
doing them an injustice to present them with a set of disparate
facts, be they dates for battles or names for rulers and not give
them anything to hang it on and not any reason to care about
it. Why should it matter? It shouldn't! It is not ok to do that.
Besides, we live in an information era in which they can look up
that kind of information if they need it if they know how to ask
the right questions. So they're learning how to learn, and they
are learning how to ask questions, the right questions, how to
access information, how to be critical thinkers.

This teacher's perspective on teaching mirrors the second major shift that came out of our curriculum committee's work that summer—a transition from a teacher-centered classroom to one that moved the students to center stage. As this teacher says, creating experiences for students so that they are actively involved in the learning process is crucial.

When I was a young teacher, I used lecture as my go-to methodology simply because that was the way I had always been taught. My focus was on the *what*, I generally tried to bridge the gap to the so what, but the *now what* was too often an afterthought. As a veteran teacher, however, on those rare occasions when I did lecture I rarely went longer than ten minutes since the focus of my class shifted from telling my students what I thought they should know to helping them arrive at their own discoveries through class discussions, group work, cooperative learning, Socratic seminars, concept maps, or other strategies, each designed to foster the second two levels of learning. Asking students to briefly write about the day's key issue before we began the discussion allowed (or perhaps forced) all students to focus their thoughts and allowed me to call on any student without fearing he or she would have nothing to say. That single practice enabled us to get to the heart of The Conversation much more quickly than before simply because the kids spent a few moments up front thinking about the critical issues of the day before our discussion even began.

As my students became more comfortable with each other and confident in their analytical skills, I even occasionally bowed out of the discussion entirely and told them I would intervene only if I saw them getting hopelessly off track. For instance, as the semester drew to a close in one of my literature classes, I asked the students to read Ernest Hemingway's "The Snows of Kilimanjaro" and Leo Tolstoy's "The Death of Ivan Ilych," two stories that deal with the death of their central character, and turned over the discussion of the authors' competing worldviews to the kids. I could have told them what the stories seem to be saying. I could have led a guided discussion that would have gotten them there. But because the kids had the opportunity to seize control of the class, they worked slowly and fitfully toward an analysis of each story that was better than anything I could have done and proved to themselves they were far better readers than they even knew. My inspiration for that lesson came from George Wood's book *A Time to Learn.*

> *Earnest Boyer, former president of the Carnegie Foundation for the Advancement of Teaching, once said that secondary schools are places "where children go to watch adults work." Wandering up and down most school hallways, it is easy to see what he means. In classroom after classroom the mode of instruction*

can be depressingly the same: one teacher standing in front of thirty or so adolescents, talking.[25]

In elaborating upon that point in the words below, Wood helped me to rethink my entire approach to teaching and spurred me to cede even more control of the class to the kids.

I knew I was doing something wrong when I left school every day tired, worn out and loaded down with grading to do, while our kids walked out full of energy and without a single book in their hands. They should work at least as hard as I do. After all, it is their education, not mine. When I figured this out, I started changing the way I teach and asking students to do more than sit, listen, and be entertained.[26]

A retired English teacher, one of the finest educators in his entire district, reached that same conclusion. Though he initially taught in an extremely conservative parochial school that emphasized worksheets and rote learning, his methodology evolved over time so that his day-to-day practice became less predictable and more centered on giving his students learning experiences and writing assignments that would challenge them to be both creative and thoughtful in their responses. Learning that mattered the most, he believed, could not best be measured simply.

Another thing I developed over the last fifteen to twenty years was I stopped doing the work for them. They come through a program in our district that is really good, but at the same time there are teachers who spend all this time coming up with worksheets or very strict rubrics. I went 180 degrees away from that because it made kids believe if I do X, Y, and Z, I can always get an A.

His shift from rote learning to more student-centered methods reflected his growing awareness of the need for relevance and depth in putting the onus for learning on the kids. There is, however, one major risk involved in moving from a teacher-centered classroom to a student-centered style of instruction, a risk that generated some resistance from part of our faculty. Because lecturing is so much more "efficient" than giving students the opportunity to arrive at an understanding through their own discovery, teachers who adopt this approach will probably be unable to include as much material as they would otherwise cover. A retired math teacher learned to live with that reality simply because he saw the value of enabling his students to work their way to their own insights.

> *When I started teaching geometry, I would have them open their textbook and show them a theorem. "OK, Theorem Number One says," and I would write it out word for word. Then I would say, "Here is how we are going to use that theorem. OK, any questions?" It was so stupid. After you have done it a while, you figure it out. "Here is a problem. If this is true, what do you know about this?" Some kid will figure something out, and then you say, "What do you know about this?" Then you can lead them up to a conclusion. "We started with this, and this is what we ended up with. You know what? Here is a theorem." They have helped create and discover the theorem. At the beginning of my career, I had no idea how to do that. It was just writing verbatim what the book said.*

Granting students the time to laboriously grind toward a breakthrough that the teacher could have presented in a few moments' time might seem counterproductive at first, but isn't that what Katharina Wilson meant when she said that in allowing students to unearth discoveries on their own, "we will have accomplished a feat far more important than the imparting of facts"?

Keep It Simple: It's Always About the Kids

Using the students' knowledge base as a starting point for learning is another essential part of a teacher's strategy, a point we emphasized as we began to define good pedagogy as a faculty. Because by the end of my career I was almost fifty years older than my students, I tried my best to stay current with their music, so that when talking about literature I could use the tunes of Bruno Mars or Miranda Lambert as a *so what* reference point rather than the Beatles' or Beach Boys' songs of my youth. To play a clip from *The Dark Knight* or *Survivor* that connected thematically with what we were reading served as a touchstone to the students' world and helped them to see that Joseph Conrad and Robert Penn Warren were not just dead white guys who knew nothing about human nature. For the last ten years of my career, I even subscribed to *Entertainment Weekly*, for one reason only—so that I would know enough about the popular television shows and movies the kids were viewing to be conversant with them without having to spend hours in a teen-filled movie theater eating stale popcorn while watching yet another superhero sequel. Knowing my students' interests enabled me to tailor our discussions to play upon their concerns and invite certain kids to contribute to the dialogue because of their special expertise. That is a strategy common among veteran teachers, as these former teachers suggest.

> *I look at the human brain, at knowledge, as a giant piece of Velcro. Every time we learn something we need to be able to attach it to something that is already lodged in our brain. So if I want to talk about some abstract concept, I need to describe it so that the students can relate to it. They need to stick it into some recognizable category that already exists in their brain. Every time they learn something, they lay a new strip of Velcro, and that makes it easier to attach the next new fact or concept to the ever-growing layers of knowledge.*

> *Teaching is kind of like wardrobing. If you buy a new suit, you have to have a hanger at home to hang it on. If you don't, the suit will fall on the ground and will not be any good, and you will not be able to use it. You probably will be less inclined to buy the tie to go with it because you are not going to use it. When I work with kids, it needs to be relevant, it needs to be accessible; abstract concepts need to be concretized and then taken back to the abstract.*

Based upon their research into how students learn, the authors of *Make It Stick* reinforce that point of view.

> *Putting new knowledge into a larger context helps learning. For example, the more of the unfolding story of human history you*

know, the more of it you can learn. And the more ways you give that story meaning, say by connecting it to your understanding of human ambition and the untidiness of fate, the better the story stays with you. Likewise, if you are trying to learn an abstraction, like the principle of angular momentum, it's easier when you ground it in something concrete that you already know, like the way a figure skater's rotation speeds up as she draws her arms to her chest.[27]

Teachers who can create word pictures or tell a story to make the abstract come alive for students enable kids to conceptualize ideas that threaten to soar over their heads. My favorite teacher in high school was a master storyteller, a man who gauged his students' attention span in his history classes with an artist's eye, turning to humanizing anecdotes about people like Catherine the Great, Oliver Cromwell, or Louis XIV or comparing them to modern day pop culture figures whenever our focus seemed to lag. More than any other teacher I ever had, he managed to make the wooden figures of our textbook seem altogether human with foibles and flaws that made them immediately recognizable. He was an expert practitioner of the strategy Ken Bain describes in *What the Best College Teachers Do*: "With carefully chosen analogies they make even the familiar seem strange and intriguing and the strange appear familiar. We found people who constantly sprinkle their classes with personal anecdotes and even emotional stories to illustrate otherwise purely intellectual topics and procedures."[28] My history teacher knew that a funny, violent, or risqué story would pique our interest, and he used his vast knowledge of the historically offbeat to make even the most uninteresting historical figures seem like our crazy aunt or uncle from Toledo. That made us more than willing to listen as he turned to the meat of the curriculum and focused on the major events he wanted us to remember. He embodied the kind of teacher described by Keith Karnok in "Thoughts on College Teaching."

It is essential that teachers use real-world examples that students can relate to. Having even the strongest understanding of the subject matter will do little good if the teacher can't explain

it in terms that students can understand. I try to have an illus-
tration or example for every major point I make and try to draw
from personal experience whenever possible. Though the use of
examples may slow down the amount of material covered, the
increased level of comprehension far outweighs the concern.[29]

One of the retired math teachers marveled at a colleague's ability to make math concepts concrete by taking a humorous approach. "You wouldn't think that math would offer much room for comedy, but this guy would have his kids in stitches through his crazy analogies and funny stories that somehow made sense in the context of explaining an equation. The kids loved him, loved his class, and learned a lot of math because of the way he taught."

Teachers who can make the abstract concrete through analogies, humor, or careful explanations of difficult material understand that one of the keys to good teaching is to keep things simple, another point we agreed upon as our curriculum committee reached its conclusions. If the brain is indeed a hodgepodge of Velcro, then teachers need to sort through those jumbled layers to find points of connection that make sense to students encountering any material for the first time. One way I tried to do that was to clearly articulate each day's goal as class began, telling the students in my writing class something like, "Today we are going to see how expert writers use figures of speech to create word pictures for their readers and inject a spark of creativity into what they write. Then you are going to practice writing metaphors and similes to ensure you know the difference and can use them effectively when you write a character sketch next week." That gave the kids a clear sense of where we were headed and removed any sense of mystery from the day's proceedings. Other teachers prefer to write the day's objectives and procedures on the board so the students know what to anticipate from the moment they walk in the door.

But there is more to keeping things simple than that. Because novice teachers tend to learn as they go, they find it hard to discern what matters and what does not and so often require too much too soon from their students. When I first began to teach writing to seniors, I set the bar way too high from the get-go, expecting kids at that level to be able to write a creative introduction, a clear thesis, well-reasoned arguments, and a thoughtful conclusion for their first paper of the year, another of the brainless expectations that marked my early days of failure. I had to learn to break each of those components into sequential parts, teaching the kids how to write each of those elements in turn before expecting them to put them all together. So when I graded their first essays of the year, I began to ignore many of the weaknesses in their papers and concentrated only on those elements of writing that we had already discussed and practiced. In *Resilience*, former Navy Seal and current Missouri governor, Eric Greitens identifies the root cause of being overly complex when trying to teach.

> *Some people love to make their lessons overly complicated. If a mentor becomes lost in his lesson, you can usually assume one of several things. One, the mentor hasn't mastered the material. Two, the mentor is trying to make himself seem important. Or three, the mentor can't remember what it was like to learn the material himself.*[30]

I was guilty as charged on all three counts. Because I had not thought through the learning process carefully enough and because I was not yet wholly conversant with the material I was teaching, I was unable to explain that information clearly enough to my students in my first few years in the classroom. I learned to simplify, simplify, simplify if I wanted to be effective, a point Robert Marzano underscores in citing Barak Rosenshine's investigation into brain research conducted in 2002.

> *The importance of teaching in small steps fits well with the findings from cognitive psychology on the limitations of our working memory. Our working memory, the place where we process information, is small. It can only handle a few bits of information at once—too much information swamps our working memory.*[31]

That is a lesson several of the veteran teachers learned as they sought to simplify their lessons as they matured in their pedagogical approach. One discovered that all that he picked up through his reading and study about the craft of teaching and about his curriculum had to be streamlined if he hoped to be effective.

There were things I did and books I read and workshops I attended [to improve]. If things worked ok, and if not I threw them away, but in that process I pared all that I did down so that the last ten years it became very simple. In doing away with all the bells and whistles for so long I realized it made it easier for every kid.

A retired drama teacher learned from hard experience that expecting her Drama I students to master all of the stagecraft necessary to convey a sense of character immediately was unrealistic, so she began to break the elements of developing a character onstage into manageable chunks by giving her students specific directions.

I would say, "This time around I want you to focus on the character's goals in those lines." Then the next time through we are going to worry about what movements would happen as a result of trying to achieve those goals. So I had to learn to break lessons down into smaller pieces and goals. . . . It was ok to do smaller things at a time. If you give it to them all at once it will overwhelm them. . . . I am a big picture person, so I probably tried to do too much early on in my teaching. Then there were more students frustrated and not feeling like they were succeeding. Then I didn't feel like I was succeeding and got frustrated.

Keeping things simple also means anticipating when and where students will need special help and designing a lesson to accommodate that reality. An upper-level math teacher knew his students would struggle with certain concepts and tailored his instruction accordingly.

I have been doing this long enough that I pretty much know where kids will struggle because I have taught the same courses for so many years. I have modified those lessons to allow more time and more examples and more direct teaching. Early in my career I had no idea where they were going to struggle. I would think, "How can you not know that?" That was a big thing that experience gave me. How to anticipate where they were going to have trouble and then heading it off before they got there. . . .

Rarely do I sense a whole class is struggling because with experi-ence I know where it is going to be harder, so we will spend more time on those ideas to head it off.

Conversely, instead of spending more time in front of a class at certain points, a former English teacher realized that approach was far less valuable than the minutes he devoted to offering kids help one on one: "When you teach writing, you can put stuff on the board all you want, you can give them models and examples, but nothing beats twenty minutes sitting next to a student and talking through what works and doesn't work. It took me much too long to learn some of those things!" In his view, all the upfront instruction he once relied on to drive his class was insignificant relative to the assistance he could offer once he sat down next to a student to offer his help. Two teachers embraced two different solutions, but each man devised a strategy to support his students when he knew they would struggle.

Questions Matter Most

Another element in keeping things simple our school began to empha-size in the last ten years of my career was to orient the structure and pace of any unit or lesson around essential questions that both guide the curricular choices teachers make and point the students to the key ideas they need to consider. Essential questions are simply those broad, concept-based, open-ended questions that raise the serious issues around which a unit will be organized and shape the readings, the problems, the media, and the discussions that will make up the daily lessons designed to address those questions. For instance, when we taught the novel *Cry, the Beloved Country*, the essential question that framed that unit was "How does the ability to forgive or the failure to forgive shape the fabric of individual lives and society as a whole?" Though we could have concentrated on showing the ways the novel is modeled on the hero's journey or concentrated on the effects of racial discrimination on the native population of South Africa in our dis-cussions and assessments, by narrowing our focus to the issue of for-giveness, we could bring in outside readings and utilize film clips to augment our consideration of that issue. Though we did in fact spend some time talking about the pattern of the hero's journey at work in the novel and about apartheid as well, neither was the focal point of our study; forgiveness was, and the bulk of our discussions centered on that theme.

Consider the value of an essential question in defining and limiting the scope of a unit. Suppose that a U.S. history teacher beginning a unit on the Civil War considers three different essential questions as possibilities for his or her unit.

- What political and military strategies did the Lincoln administration employ to guide the North to victory in the Civil War?
- Was the Civil War brought on primarily by a dispute between North and South over states' rights or slavery?
- Why do some historians argue that though the South lost the Civil War on the battlefield, it won the war legally, legislatively, and culturally for the next hundred years?

Each of these questions offers a myriad of opportunities for fruitful study and interesting conversations, but the focal point of each is radically different. By choosing any one of the three, the teacher will necessarily limit what she addresses and will select readings and create learning experiences unique to that question alone. In a sense, an essential question serves as an organizing principle around which a unit or lesson revolves, as Grant Wiggins suggests: "The aim is to establish clear inquiry priorities within a course around which facts are learned."[32]

During my last year at my school, I mentored three young teachers just beginning their careers as educators. Because of a major change in the curriculum of the courses they taught, they had no preexisting essential questions to frame their curriculum, so each struggled to define the priorities that would shape what he or she taught. Due to their inexperience, the absence of essential questions proved terribly frustrating to all of them since they found it difficult to gauge what their emphases should be and realized that their first few units meandered from day to day with no controlling idea to tie each disparate lesson together. Part of my job as a mentor, then, became to help them

write the essential questions that would serve as a guiding, unifying principle for each unit. As the year unfolded and they became more familiar with the curriculum, they were increasingly able to write the kinds of questions that would both get at the heart of the material and excite the kids with the possibilities that those questions raised. Their essential questions became a springboard for open-ended inquiry, ones designed to provoke and evoke curiosity while providing an organizing structure for each unit. If ever I doubted the value of taking the time to write essential questions, my experience with those three young teachers convinced me of their merit once and for all.

Though the principles described above are far from comprehensive, they became the points of emphasis that emerged from the two years our committee spent studying the art and science of teaching. Though we did not know it at the time, our conclusions proved remarkably congruent with the recommendations Linda Darling-Hammond offered when she wrote that students learn best when their teachers consistently practice certain identifiable behaviors.

- They connect new ideas to what students already know.
- They allow students to apply their knowledge to real world problems.
- They articulate clear goals to their students.
- They give ample time for their students to practice new skills.
- They use their own interests and strengths to generate interest within their students.[33]

In the years that followed and as those ideas took root, we began to emphasize other factors like backward design, curriculum mapping, and a focus on defining literacy in each discipline, but to claim that we reached the same level of buy-in in those areas as we did in the ones Darling-Hammond mentions would be a lie. We made progress on each front, but the slow adaptors continued to drag their heels to the end. Yet the comment one of the graduating seniors made in his *Calvin and Hobbes* reflection suggests that we did make real progress in embedding the initial work of our curriculum committee into the life of the school.

One of my favorite things about school is the "What? So What? Now What?" curriculum basis. Because of this, my metaphor [for effective teaching] is a fire. A fire must have a good base. This is the "What?" phase. Lighting the fire is the "So what?" phase, as you start to begin to realize impacts of certain topics. The "Now what?" phase is the sparks—what sparks action and change.

Trying to define good teaching exhaustively is a fool's mission. Because all teachers have their strengths, all students are unique, and each school faces a special set of challenges, the eureka moment in which the final answer to solving our educational woes is found is as elusive today as it was in the 1920s when Charles Elmer Holley wrote his report. Teachers, let alone schools, cannot be like a starting pitcher with only one pitch. The greatest curveball in the world will not suffice since major league hitters will quickly learn to adjust. In the same way, a teacher—or a school—that relies on one foolproof approach will flounder because each student is so different. The principles described above helped me improve and helped our school improve, but there is far more to good teaching than can be captured in a few critical concepts. Though he taught for more than thirty-five years and was widely respected for his teaching and coaching excellence, one of the retired teachers says he never really felt that he had arrived: "I never thought that. I thought, 'I want to be good at this,' but there was always the thought that you'll never get everybody, and that niggles at you. I never thought of it that way." Excellent teaching is an elusive target because students are unpredictable, and teachers are too. So much of what goes on in a classroom is serendipitous, a surprise to the teacher who thinks he or she is going *here* with a lesson and instead goes *there*, as one teacher remembers.

I loved jazz and I loved the days when things happened that I never could have imagined. I could feel myself like a jazz musician picking up a theme from a student and playing with it. It's magic, this kind of jazz improv. You start with a theme and all of a sudden you are transcending sitting here in a classroom. You are soaring. Those are magic moments.

Those "magic moments" occur most often when teachers see the students' questions as more important than their own and recognize that they are there to stir their students' sense of curiosity and awaken a desire within them to know more. We may not always do that well, but as this student attests, when teachers are willing to step aside for the sake of their students, sometimes the magic does happen.

> *My best experiences here have been like running a relay race. At the beginning of the school year, the teacher did most of the work, teaching us, guiding us, and giving us the foundation for our journey. Then the best teachers handed the baton to the students and let us do the running, the figuring out, the wrestling with deep and uncomfortable questions. They were always there to help us and guide us again, to take the baton and help us out for awhile, but it was always back in our hands again afterward because the class wasn't about the information; it was about us and the men and women we would someday become.*

Isn't that the way it should be? If all schools in America could achieve those results, the crisis in education would be over at last.

Reflections

1. Who are the educational thinkers who matter to you? How have they influenced your beliefs and practices about teaching?
2. To what degree do you think teaching is an art? To what degree is it a science? Which matters more?
3. Is it more important to you that students leave your class each day/at the end of the year with information or with questions? Why?
4. What would it look like in your class if you "stopped doing the work for them"? What would be gained? What would be lost?
5. Have you written essential questions for each of your units? How would you benefit if you took the time to do so? How would your students benefit?

Action Items

1. What is the *so what* for tomorrow's lesson? What is the *now what*? How will the answers to these questions affect the way you teach it?

2. What is the *so what* for the unit you are presently teaching? What is the *now what*? How will the answers to these questions affect the way you teach it?

3. Consider the information in your curriculum that your students struggle with the most. How can you chunk the information in that unit/lesson so that your students can master it most efficiently and easily?

4. Write the essential questions for your next unit so that you have a clear idea of exactly what you want to accomplish with your students.

Chapter Five
Defining How to Improve

Though wasting time is a highly practiced art form for most high school kids, the biggest waste of time I experienced during my sophomore year came not from watching reruns of *The Beverly Hillbillies* or sleeping till noon on weekends; it came instead every sixth hour when I sat through the most useless study hall in the history of secondary education. Mr. Engel (not his real name) was a man in his sixties marking time until retirement who had zero ability to control the chaos that swirled through the room each day as he made absolutely no attempt to keep the room quiet. If a group of friends wanted to catch up on the latest gossip, his study hall was the place to be. If pitchers on the baseball team wanted to keep their arm loose for the spring, this classroom was the perfect venue because they could hurl spit wads with impunity for fifty-five minutes a day. The word was out: Want to get out of your seat and wander up and down the rows of desks to talk to the hot girl or guy you have your eye on? Come to Mr. Engel's study hall. Want to make fun of the fat kid or the skinny kid or the kid with acne? Come to Mr. Engel's study hall. Nobody was safe, nobody could concentrate, nobody could get any work done at all. Though I was hardly the most diligent student in the school, even I sat frustrated and peeved day after day because of the bedlam dominating the room. The class was a farce, the period was a waste, and Mr. Engel was invisible.

While serving on the student newspaper staff a year later, I was assigned a story that required me to search the school archives to find out what it had been like to go to our high school twenty-five years before. As I paged through old yearbooks and back issues of the school paper marveling at the outdated fashions and once trendy hairstyles, I was struck by something far more astonishing: Three times in the 1940s Mr. Engel had been voted Most Outstanding Teacher by the student body. Twice he had been named runner-up. The fact that the man I considered an embarrassment had once been the most highly respected teacher on the faculty tore my heart to shreds.

This man was once a superb teacher, was once a beloved, honored member of the faculty. Now he was barely hanging on, wholly unable to control a roomful of fifteen-year-olds for fifty-five minutes and reduced to supervising study hall rather than teaching history as he had done for so long. Because even then I knew I wanted to teach, his example loomed as a stark warning. This man had been a model teacher, gifted and revered, but somehow, somewhere, his career had gone off the tracks. How did he lose the ability to stand before a room full of teenagers while commanding their respect and affection? What caused him to stagnate? What caused him to give up? These were questions I could not answer then and still cannot. But I have always regarded Mr. Engel as a personal cautionary tale, a constant reminder that once I became a teacher I could not afford to stand still and needed to maintain the drive to excel to my final day in the classroom.

Mr. Engel's example haunted me throughout my career, filled me with a sense that self-awareness is a vital part of any teacher's repertoire, and showed me that those who choose to rest on their laurels are doing their students a terrible disservice. One of the retired teachers could have been speaking for any teacher committed to excellence when he said, "I wanted to be the best. Anybody can take kids through fifty-five minutes of class time, but if I couldn't give them my best, I was my own worst critic. I would have to look myself in the face and say, 'Hey you could have done a much better job.'"

That drive to pursue continual improvement is one of the hallmarks of truly great teachers. Perhaps they are driven by ego, or perhaps they are driven by a sense of calling to serve their students well, but a refusal to settle into respectable mediocrity is crucial for those who want to hold onto their idealistic dreams of what education should be. But with that choice comes a fair measure of pain, as a former English teacher says: "I had to anguish about teaching before I could do it. If you don't anguish about it and avoid the confrontation with yourself, I think you become a bit of a fraudulent teacher." Getting better means hard work—lots of it. Getting better means making the time to reflect upon and dissect each lesson, taking careful notes at the close of a unit to write down all that worked and all that did not so that next year will be an improvement. In fact, as I finished a unit, I learned to write an analysis of it so that if and when I returned to that novel or essay assignment, I would have an on-the-spot assessment of what had gone well and what had gone poorly. Rather than waiting a year or more and trying to piece together the ups and downs of an old unit based upon hazy memories of what had gone before, I had a record of my successes and failures to use as a starting point upon which to build. Growing as a teacher means facing one's failures head-on, not running from them, says one retired math teacher: "Being able to look yourself in the mirror and ask why it's not working is an important part of being a teacher. Brutal honesty. Don't make excuses. Don't hold back. How can I get better tomorrow?"

The impulse to coast on last year's lesson or to succumb to the temptation to get by on the same old test that has worked for the past five years is a battle that every teacher faces. But the truth is that, unlike years past, many schools today have so fully integrated a culture of improvement into the DNA of the building that those who want to grow are more often than not surrounded by like-minded others who will support them every step of the way. In an age in which induction programs for new teachers are standard fare and professional learning communities designed to build a climate of collaboration are common, the push to improve is part of the lifeblood of many schools. Certainly educators committed to excellence should avoid being dragged down by those old guard teachers uninterested in change who exist in every building, but teachers today seeking to grow in their craft have access to programs and like-minded colleagues that can smooth the path to competence in the classroom.

The Way It Was

That has not always been the case. It is easy to forget just how poorly even good schools greeted new teachers in the not-too-distant past. When I was hired for my first job in 1973, here is how I was welcomed.

- Along with the other new teachers, I reported to school a half day ahead of the returning teachers and was given a quick run through of discipline procedures, attendance policies, and lunchroom supervision duties.
- As part of the day-and-a-half orientation with the rest of the faculty, I was handed my textbooks, given my room keys, and introduced to the other members of my department, including my department chair.
- I met for the first time the woman with whom I would team-teach for two periods a day.
- I was assigned three preps in three different classrooms with thirty or more students in each of my individual classes and more than sixty in each of the classes I would team-teach.
- I was given no curriculum apart from the textbooks—no course goals, no learning objectives, no curriculum maps, no old assessments or handouts or lesson plans.

The teachers in my department were friendly, the principal was encouraging, but the culture of the school was one in which teachers were left to figure it out for themselves. Though the intention behind asking me to team-teach was sound in that doing so would theoretically allow me to collaborate with a veteran teacher, her view of teaching had hardened through years and years of experience, and she had little interest in trying anything new. She was nice, she was kind, but it was a long and brutal year.

And for the most part, that experience was the norm for most teachers until the last dozen or so years. None of the retired teachers with whom I spoke was greeted with a formal induction or mentoring process and was instead largely left to grope his or her way toward competence through sheer willpower and effort. This teacher's experience was typical.

> I just remember how hard it was. I didn't know anything, so I had to learn the subject; I had to learn how to teach. I was coaching two sports, and in those days they handed you a book and said, "You're the teacher." That was literally how it worked. And at my second school it was, "Here's the world history book."

> *Who am I supposed to talk to? There were good teachers in the*
> *building, but they weren't in our department.*

This former teacher captures the attitude toward new teachers that prevailed in most schools until recently: "It was sink or swim. Here is your schedule, here are your textbooks, here is your room, you've been trained to be a teacher, go teach. Figure it out." Some of the retired teachers, however, did benefit from the help of colleagues who did what they could to assist despite the lack of a formal mentoring program.

> *There was no program. But was I mentored? Absolutely. I think*
> *it was because I was the fair-haired boy. Everybody I taught*
> *with were my former teachers. My senior teacher was a guy who*
> *took me under his wing. My department chair had been my*
> *sophomore English teacher. I made a lot of mistakes, mistakes*
> *that could have gotten me fired. There were a lot of young teach-*
> *ers. It was a new school we had just opened up, so we had a lot*
> *of help. There were older teachers who had been there since the*
> *forties, and here we were coming in as a whole group of young*
> *teachers, so we had each other to watch after, and we had older*
> *teachers who liked us and gave us guidance.*

In my second school, I was helped immensely by Patrick Berger, a veteran teacher who could not have been more generous. Because our department was comprised of a group of young but willing beginners, he treated us as family and fought for us when the administration seemed oblivious to the special concerns of the department. His openness to sharing ideas created a climate in which we felt free to borrow and adapt each other's materials, and the atmosphere he fostered helped make that department one of the strongest in the school. A former teacher who was part of that department remembers what it was like to work in such a supporting environment: "Pat and the people . . . that I worked with were incredible. I still remember the things we did to make learning enjoyable and valuable at the same time. Guys like you and Jim Schmuck and Nick Otten and Barb Harris. Pat was great."

Teachers lucky enough to land in such a situation are fortunate, but the path to classroom excellence is still a long, hard pull. To say it again, I was *shocked* in my first few years at the sheer volume of grading and the relentless grind of lesson planning. There were no shortcuts. Reading the books I would teach and researching the background necessary to put each novel or play in context took more hours than I care to recall. My wife is still upset that when we were engaged I would tell her I could not see her every night because I had too much work to do. And my experience was hardly exceptional; endless hours of study are part of the routine that any good teacher must accept. Here is how one former teacher remembers his career.

> *You have to be willing to put in time to make yourself better. Not because the administrator tells you to do it but because you want to do it. I want to see signs that a teacher is never going to feel satisfied to say, "Okay, I can use these notes for the next twenty years or I can teach this novel for the next twenty years because I've got it down lockstep." You have to constantly have the courage and drive to search out new ways of doing what you did today to make it better tomorrow or next year. You have to have that passion, that drive, to want to be with the stuff that makes you as a teacher stronger.*

Finding Your Yoda

One way young teachers can learn how to do their job well is simply to keep their ears open. When a Spanish teacher left our school five years after beginning his career with us, he stopped by my room on the last day of final exams to thank me for mentoring him. Perplexed because I had never served as his mentor and so had no idea what he was talking about, he said that during the five years we had eaten lunch together he had been a silent witness to the many conversations that those with whom we ate had about teaching. Through those discussions, he said, he had established a set of principles about pedagogy and classroom management that had helped him figure out how to teach. That kind of informal mentoring is a by-product of the casual conversations available to anyone who cares to ask questions and let the veteran teachers speak. For those with ears to hear, the path to improvement is available as part of the routine of the school day, says one retired teacher, who looked to the veterans in his department for inspiration early on.

> *At lunchtime conversations, in hallway conversations and after school chitchat these folks were not dialing it in; these folks strove to get better. It wasn't necessarily explicit . . . but if you had a question you could go to them without embarrassment or hindrance, without any sense that you were any kind of lesser guy, a "Why are you asking me this?" mentality. I was always looking for tomorrow's lesson plan or who can do it better. They were mentors in the sense that though they took their position seriously, they didn't take themselves seriously.*

But because they are reluctant to expose their vulnerability, some novice teachers are slow to ask for help, a point of frustration for one of the teachers with whom I spoke: "It amazed me how seldom the new teachers in our building asked for advice about how to teach. We wanted to help, we made the offer, but it was almost as if they thought if they asked we would look down on them." An answer for new teachers in schools without formal mentoring programs, therefore, is to seek help; whatever the risk of confessing their ignorance, struggling teachers will likely find a sympathetic audience from any longtime teacher who remembers the stress of year one. That is the advice one of the former teachers offers in describing his formula for helping young teachers succeed.

> *The first advice I would give them is learn from the best. Find out who the really great teachers are in your school and your community. Invite them to lunch, have a cup of coffee with them on a regular basis, visit their school, watch them teach, find out what good teaching is all about.*

A variation of that formula helped a newly retired math teacher to flourish when he was first hired at a school that had no formal mentoring program.

> *I had Art Stout, which was as good a mentoring program as you could possibly get. Art was just a father figure to all the young*

*teachers in the math department. . . . He would come down to
your room and just talk. He would give you hints about how
to do stuff. He would talk about how to relate to kids, particularly how you need to keep your distance from the sixteen- to
seventeen-year-old girls. . . . He talked to me about how I have
to maintain professional distance. He would talk to me about
developing lesson plans and how to teach certain things. We
would talk about how you would do different lessons with different levels of kids.*

Empathetic teachers like Art Stout can be found in every building.
Although the culture of some schools even at this late date might leave
young teachers feeling isolated, every school has its wise heads, men
and women who are invested in helping the next generation of teachers. Taking the ideas of those veteran teachers and incorporating them
into his own lessons is something that one retired teacher learned early
in the game: "I developed a Robin Hood complex—you rob from the
rich, you pull it all in. You may not do it exactly the same way another
person would—you give your own twist to it—but at the same time
you are listening and observing."

The Curse of Hollywood

In sessions she led with our faculty in her role as director of teaching
and learning at my former school, Cindy Zavaglia pointed out another
barrier new teachers face in trying to improve: Hollywood is obsessed
with the myth of the superstar teacher and creates the expectation that
the great teacher is the one who fights the battle alone. Think about
the traditional movies or television shows about education. A trou-
bled group of students lacks focus and direction until the right teacher
perseveres in opening their eyes to the beauty of learning and the possibilities of who they might be. Whether it is John Keating in *Dead
Poets Society*, Eric Taylor in *Friday Night Lights*, Louanne Johnson in
Dangerous Minds, or Mark Thackeray in *To Sir with Love*, one coura-
geous teacher defies convention and forges a creative path to learning
that captures the minds of the students and changes their lives forever.
Kids who would have gone to jail or to the streets come alive, go to

Harvard, commit to a career in astrophysics and negotiate an end to the Arab-Israeli divide all because of one heroic man or woman in the classroom.

An extreme example is *Mr. Holland's Opus*, a film in which Mr. Holland's career culminates in a final tribute to his dedication produced by his former students—a public performance of his masterpiece, a composition he has labored over for years but that has never been performed before an audience. The film ends with Mr. Holland directing his opus while, as the film makes clear, his grateful students—his life's real work—play on in homage to his commitment to them. Some teachers love that movie. It is moving, it is inspirational, and it has the ultimate happy ending. In its sappy sentimentality, however, it makes others want to swig a bottle of gin and sleep away the weekend in an alcohol-fueled coma.

Whatever its faults, the movie does contain one scene that strikes at the core of how teachers improve. Watching Mr. Holland's marching band stumble around the field ineptly, the football coach, Bill Meister, offers to teach the kids how to march if Mr. Holland will accept the challenge of helping a struggling student by allowing him to play drums in the band despite his utter lack of rhythm. Totally frustrated by the student's inability to find the beat after weeks of trying, Mr. Holland turns to Coach Meister and says that it is time to give up—this student just cannot learn. Coach Meister's response is pointed: "Then you are a lousy teacher." Any student can learn, the coach says, if only Mr. Holland will try to get inside his head to understand how to reach him. In an ensuing montage, Mr. Holland experiments with a wide range of creative approaches designed to help the student get on track, succeeding only after even more failure and ever more radical attempts to help the young man find his way.

Three key principles emerge from this scene. The first is that Coach Meister will not allow Mr. Holland to give up. He holds Mr. Holland accountable, challenges his competence, and refuses to let him quit. The second is that Mr. Holland tries method after method before the concept clicks, and the student triumphs at last. It bears repeating—teaching doesn't stop until the student actually learns something. The third cuts to the heart of the ideal culture of a school. Two teachers work together, two teachers collaborate, calling on each other's strengths to meet the needs of two different kinds of students. By trading on each teacher's expertise, the band learns to march, and the student learns to play the drums in rhythm. The lone superstar is out. Two teachers working side by side is in.

Getting Better Together

The merits of collaboration have been embraced by district after district in recent years as school leaders have begun to understand the value of asking teachers to work together. By generating common lesson plans, assessments, and activities, teachers guarantee that all students taking Algebra II or American Lit. will share roughly the same experience and face the same level of difficulty on tests and other assignments.

Our school was late to the table in this regard. As recently as ten years ago, those teaching the same class on the same grade level had broad freedom to design their own curricula, choose their own texts, and write their own tests independently of one another. That began to change only when a frustrated father called one day to complain about the radically different experience his son was having in U.S. History after switching from one teacher to another at the semester. Teacher number one lectured all hour each day, gave tests heavy on essays and short answers, and ended the first semester with his unit on the Civil War. Teacher number two was into PowerPoint presentations, gave tests heavy on true-false and multiple-choice questions, and began the second semester with his unit on the Civil War. The teachers' classrooms were no more than fifty feet apart, yet each man did his thing with no regard to what his colleague was doing or what the students needed. Challenged by the father's justifiable bewilderment, I had no good answer for the lack of communication and cooperation between teachers in the same department. I could only promise that things would change.

And change they did. Within a year the teachers agreed upon the texts they would jointly use, coordinated the style and timing of their tests, and adopted a bit of each other's pedagogical methodology to ensure that students in both classes had a largely similar experience. The problem was not unique to our school. A retired principal, one who valued the importance of allowing his teachers to take time for

The Conversation, recalls seeing the danger that giving teachers total autonomy posed when observing two world history teachers the week before second semester final exams.

> *I walked into one teacher's classroom and he was doing Napoleon, and across the hall another was doing Nazi Germany in the same level world history class. . . . As the line goes, if there are two twins in the school, they should have roughly the same experience. I was never a fanatic about that, but you cannot have one kid get to Napoleon while the other kid is getting to World War II. So we started having conversations about common curriculum. These kids cannot have such vastly different experiences in the classroom.*

Collaboration between teachers takes time and of course can never be entirely seamless. Because students learn at different rates and because no teacher can anticipate when The Conversation will take his class in a direction he did not anticipate, no group of teachers can move forward in rigid lockstep. But in collaborating, teachers are able to build upon each other's strengths, divide the workload in preparing tests and handouts, and inspire one another's creative juices by challenging the assumptions each brings to the table. After teaching a senior-level English class solo for at least a decade in the pre-collaboration days, I began to rethink that course late in my career through working with a teacher in his third year in education. Because he brought a fresh pair of eyes to the curriculum and the perspective of another generation, he was able to make a number of suggestions to improve the course that energized the students and made me a better teacher. If I actually did achieve my goal of continuing to grow as a teacher till the last day of my career, that young teacher deserves much of the credit. Our students gained through our collective wisdom, and because the other teacher and I shared the responsibility for creating writing assignments, tests, and handouts, neither of us had to spend the time that would have been required had we been working alone.

A retired English teacher recalls that a humanities class taught collaboratively with two other teachers was one of the highlights of his career. Asked by his principal to work with a history and an art teacher to design and teach the class, he recalls what a positive experience that class proved to be for students and teachers alike.

> *We three coordinated what we were doing with each other so that what I was teaching in the literature coordinated with the historical time frame, which also reflected the art that was coming out of that period. It was outstanding. It was fun to teach, the kids enjoyed it. . . . We worked together, we coordinated together, we met together, we went to workshops together. We did all kinds of things together. It was really fabulous, and it was a prototype. . . . That was a coordinated program that was really, really interesting. The kids really enjoyed it because if I needed two hours to do something I used two hours, and then I gave the time back for something else.*

A retired business teacher learned the value of collaboration out of necessity well into his career when his school got its first generation of classroom computers.

> *In about 1980/81, we got our first Apple computers. . . . We got five Apple IIs, and we actually built a wall that separated the back parts of the room and put glass there so we could lock them up. We looked at each other and said, "What does this machine even do? How is this going to make a difference to us and to our kids? What are we even going to do with this?" There was no curriculum. "What do you mean this is a floppy disk? What does that even mean? It does what? You put it in there and it does what? What is word processing? What is a database? You can create spreadsheets and reports?" The three of us just started writing curriculum, and then we'd teach ourselves. We would teach the same course, so we'd try something, and we would say, "Hey this worked pretty well today. Or I tried this and it didn't work very well." Three of us worked like dogs trying to write curriculum, write activities and integrate this thing into our teaching.*

That experience, he says, was one of the richest of his professional career and gave him a sense of the power of a collaborative professional learning community years before he ever even heard the term.

Although the school did not set aside time for the members of this team to meet together, they convened before and after school, at lunch, and even during the summer to map out their approach to integrating computers into the classroom. Finding the time to meet for collaboration in a school that does not build that time into the schedule is difficult when one of the teachers in a PLC coaches the debate team and another coaches cross country, but most teachers who work in a collaborative community would argue that carving out that time is vital.

That's because working together to sharpen each other's thinking is a critical component in the professional growth of an educator. Even in schools in which PLCs are not part of the culture, like-minded teachers can still make collaboration a priority. "It's tough, I know," says one of the retired teachers. "Time is always a premium." But collegiality, cooperation, and shared expertise are so important that ignoring the opportunities to grow by failing to work together means that a new teacher has to figure out how to grade an essay, how to evaluate a portfolio, how to design a test, and how to frame a lesson in isolation. As one who spent untold hours in the library working alone to develop the background information and lesson plans I would use in the classroom, I can attest that life became much simpler when my colleagues came alongside to share the workload, pool our creative ideas, and steer the conversation in directions I would never have thought of on my own. Here is another benefit to collaboration: teachers who work together model the ideal of being lifelong learners and pave the way for their students to follow along, as Roland Barth suggests in *Learning by Heart.*

> *Ultimately there are two kinds of schools: learning enriched schools and learning impoverished schools. I have yet to see a school where the learning curves . . . of the adults were steep upward and those of the students were not. Teachers and students go hand in hand as learners . . . or they don't go at all.*[1]

Teachers who work jointly play upon one another's strengths. One of the women with whom I was part of a three-person PLC was a genius at designing handouts that enabled students to structure their essays easily and clearly. Her eye for detail was an immense aid in determining ways to help our students understand how and why the parts of an essay fit together. I was good at curriculum design and finding examples of effective writing to serve as models for our students. The third member of our team was both the voice of reason who kept our meetings moving forward and so widely read that he discovered story and essay options for our curriculum that neither the first teacher nor I would have found. So I was good at the big picture, she was good with the specifics, and the third teacher was good at finding materials that would flesh out what we were trying to do. Because our strengths complemented each other's nicely, our students benefited, and we each became better. One of the teachers I spoke to had the same experience when she became part of a PLC.

> You can't do this in isolation. . . . And I don't just mean a casual lunchtime conversation. We do serious work around here. We talk about what the kids are doing and what they are missing and how best to get them to master those important skills. You have to have a culture of thoughtful grown-ups who do the same kinds of things we expect our kids to do, like reflect, analyze, consider, examine, revise, study, assess, ditch. It is kind of like making the reintellectualization of teaching part of our active work.

It's Never Easy

Professional learning communities are certainly not a panacea. A problem with collaboration, of course, is that successful cooperation is dependent upon the ability of a group of teachers to agree upon what should be taught and how it should be assessed. Conflicting philosophical agendas or differences in curricular priorities can derail what could have been a successful partnership. Another barrier to meaningful collaboration is the personalities and egos of those attempting to work together. Teachers who don't get along or whose teaching styles clash find it hard to put aside their own approach to compromise with a colleague they don't really want to work with in the first place. Human nature gets in the way of a department chair's perfectly designed plan to implement PLCs simply because two temperaments do not click. Some teachers resent being asked—or required—to work with others because they enjoy the independence that has long been the traditional hallmark of curriculum design, and still others feel their own teaching style will be subsumed by groupthink as they are asked to adapt to another person's methodology. One of the retired teachers, who was himself a proponent of collaborative teaching, agrees that teachers must remain true to their own instincts even when they incorporate their colleagues' methodology into what they do.

> *Find your identity as a teacher—what works for you. Because our personalities are different, what works for the very best teacher may not work for you. You have to learn from different people and find your rhythm, your personality. . . . You have to find who you are and play to your strengths.*

But whatever the drawbacks, the benefits of working and learning together proved to be one of the most helpful changes that occurred in the culture of the school in which I worked and an impetus to my growth as a teacher as well. Tom Carroll captured the essence of our experience in "The Next Generation of Learning Teams" published in *Phi Delta Kappan*: "Quality teaching is not an individual accomplishment, it is the result of a collaborative culture that empowers teachers to team up to improve student learning beyond what any one of them can achieve alone."[2] Because I had a place to ask questions, because I had colleagues who could challenge and sharpen my thinking, because I worked with teachers who had skills and knew information I did not, because I served on a team willing to share the burden, and because we laughed together and encouraged one another, the time we spent in a PLC enriched each of us and enriched our students as well.

What keeps a teacher energized for thirty or forty years? Doing the same lessons in the same order with the same worksheets and the same assessments doesn't get it done. Never standing still, always seeking a new way to connect an abstract idea to the world of the kids, forever maintaining a thirst to learn more and more and more—that's the road to a long and fulfilling career. As one of my colleagues used to say, "Are you going to have one year of experience thirty times or thirty years of experience one year at a time?" Think of the difference it would make in the lives of all kinds of students if every teacher adopted the attitude of this educator: "The day that I find myself stagnating is the day I need to get out of teaching. There are plenty of teachers marking time until they put in their thirty years, but I pray to God I am never one of them." And it is not just the students who suffer when a burned-out teacher stays too long. Here is the viewpoint of a newly retired teacher about the need to keep the internal fires stoked:

If you don't love this profession, get out now and go do something else, please! We have all seen those people who have stuck it out and they are just making it miserable for everybody. Their colleagues can't stand working with them. When I started, we had some of those older teachers, and we just needed them to check out.

That says it well. Mr. Engel was the touchstone of my career for all the wrong reasons, and, in fact, he was let go at the end of that miserable year I spent in his class. Somehow this once great teacher lost his fire, and his students paid the price. The thirst for constant improvement drives the best teachers, and those who spend their careers asking, "How can I do this better?" will be jazzed to the very end. For all the talk about education reform current in the public arena, unless teachers are committed to the craft and to the kids, all the money in the world will make little difference. Those who continue to grow and embrace the enormity of what they do bring more meaningful reform to the classroom than anyone in Washington can ever imagine.

Reflections

1. Does your school foster a culture of collaboration? If so, what help do you most need from those with whom you meet to ensure your continued growth as an educator?
2. If not, are there like-minded teachers in your building who are willing to collaborate to build a stronger curriculum? How will you carve out time in your schedules to make that happen?

3. What are your greatest strengths as a teacher? In what areas do you most need to improve? Who in your building can best help you to do so?

4. Who are the teachers in your school who have given up? Why did they become so jaded? What effect does their negative attitude have on the rest of the faculty?

Action Items

1. Does your school have a mentoring program in place? If so, what five priorities do you most want your mentor to help you with this year?

2. If not, what steps can you take to identify someone in your building who would be willing to meet with you regularly to help you grow professionally?

3. What teacher in your school has mastered an element of teaching—classroom management, creative lesson plans, systems and procedures—that you struggle with? Ask that teacher to meet with you to help you improve in that area.

Chapter Six
Why Relationships Matter

To say that the relationship between a teacher and his or her students matters is axiomatic, but if I have learned anything in the years I have spent in the classroom, it is that nothing matters more. The old cliché that students do not care what their teacher knows until they know their teacher cares is no less true for being repeated so often. Though it took me years to figure it out, a lot of students—probably most students—are scared when they walk into the classroom on the first day of school, and if a teacher cannot quickly break through the anxiety-induced barriers of self-protection that students erect, then it will be difficult for any student to flourish in that class. Though he was speaking about elementary-aged children when he wrote *How Children Fail* in the 1970s, John Holt's words apply to teenagers to some degree as well.

> *What is most surprising of all is how much fear there is in school. Why is so little said about it? Perhaps most people do not recognize fear in children when they see it. They can read the grossest signs of fear; they know what the trouble is when a child clings howling to his mother; but the subtler signs of fear escape them. It is these signs, in children's faces, voices, and gestures, in their movements and ways of working, that tell me plainly that most children in school are scared most of the time, many of them very scared. Like good soldiers, they control their fears, live with them, and adjust themselves to them. But the trouble is, and here is a vital difference between school and war, that the adjustments children make to their fears are almost wholly*

> *bad, destructive of their intelligence and capacity. The scared*
> *fighter may be the best fighter, but the scared learner is always*
> *a poor learner.*[1]

Middle school and high school kids do not cling to their mother's leg, and let's hope none of them howl at the thought of walking into their first-hour class, but any teacher paying any attention at all does not have to look very hard to see evidence that a lot of adolescents fear looking stupid or having their ignorance exposed in front of their peers. Try asking a tough question, then check the lack of eye contact as kids duck their heads to avoid being called on; that says everything a teacher needs to know about most students' unwillingness to take a chance on being wrong. This reluctance to take risks became dramatically clear to me in watching the behavior of one of the finest students I have ever taught. This young man (let's call him Brian) walked into my first hour AP Literature class his senior year with quite a reputation. He carried a stratospheric GPA and had scored a five on the four AP tests he had taken his junior year. Since my class was almost entirely discussion based, I expected Brian to star in classroom debates or at least to contribute significantly. Instead, he sat nearly mute, and whenever I asked him a question, a strange dynamic occurred; the other kids, who had all been in many classes with Brian throughout their years in high school, would sit up, look at him expectantly, and await what they knew would be his well-practiced response. Turning bright red, he would mumble, "I don't have anything to add." The problem was never that Brian had failed to read the assigned novels or short stories. If I forced him to actually say something, he almost always was on target, and his written work was essentially flawless with both a good command of the text and a thoughtful response to it. He earned a high A in my class, scored a five on the AP Literature exam, and did the same on the three other AP tests he took his senior year. So it was not as if Brian truly had nothing to contribute. Not until the night he graduated did I finally find out why Brian had been so unexpectedly reluctant to speak. As the class valedictorian, he addressed the audience at commencement and confessed that his number one priority in every class he took in high school was to avoid looking stupid. This brilliant young man, this young man who earned a full ride to a high-profile university and who outshone his classmates in terms of sheer brainpower was so uncertain of his academic ability that he sought to hide out in all of his classes throughout four years of high school, and probably for years before that. As I sat listening to Brian that night, the reality that his experience was far from unique sank in, and though it was not as if the importance of creating a safe harbor in the classroom was a revelation, that was the moment I realized that doing so was crucial to helping students become comfortable enough to let loose in front of their peers. As teachers, we had failed Brian badly in convincing him that a wrong answer was an indictment of his IQ. Somehow we had been unable to convince Brian that being wrong is a necessary component of learning, that testing hypotheses, floating trial balloons, or throwing out a wild idea is what truly creative people do. Bob Sullo recognizes the negative impact that fear like Brian's can have on student achievement in *The Motivated Student*.

> *Remember that all new learning requires that students become vulnerable and take a risk as they move out of their comfort zones. When students are afraid, they focus on self-preservation rather than the acquisition of new knowledge and the development of new skills. By removing fear from the classroom, you encourage your students to take risks and learn more.*[2]

Kids are scared, and it is a teacher's job to alleviate that anxiety by creating a climate in which it is okay to take risks without fear of ridicule, embarrassment, or especially, humiliation.

Being Liked Isn't the Goal

Some teachers do that in all the wrong ways. When I was a very young teacher, I cared too much that my students liked me and insinuated myself into their personal lives far more than I should have. Though I had no business giving some of my students dating advice, I did so (highly ironic since my social life was as barren as the Gobi Desert) and spent way too much time talking about my personal life in class. That was my immaturity screaming for their approval, and if I have one regret about my early years—besides my basic incompetence—

that would be it. It was only in my third year of teaching when a senior girl asked me out on a date that I realized I was being too familiar, and I pulled back irrevocably after that day. Being cool is not what being a teacher is about, and whatever fantasies I ever harbored about being cool vanished once and for all the moment that young woman approached me because of my failure to establish appropriate limits.

Though my behavior went too far, I never crossed any serious lines that endangered a student or threatened my career. But some teachers so earnestly seek the approval of their students—or seek to take advantage of them—that they exercise terrible judgment and face the consequences of dismissal or even criminal action. Every school district can point to examples of teachers who have sought out relationships that were inappropriate, so much so that it is difficult to go even a month without news of yet another teacher-student sex scandal. Those cases cannot possibly end well. But the bad choices teachers make can often take other forms. My career had barely begun when I first encountered a pathetic example of a teacher who did not know where to draw the line. That one didn't end well either.

Sometime during the spring semester of my second year as a teacher, a strange pattern began to develop involving four eighth-grade boys in my third-period English class. At least two days a week, these boys would come seven or eight minutes late to class with a pass from their industrial arts teacher asking that they be excused because they had stayed late to clean up the mess they had made while working on whatever project they had been assigned. At first I let this go, but when one pass turned into two, then three, then eight and ten, I became upset that this teacher so consistently let his students intrude upon my time. As a young teacher I was reluctant to confront a man in his forties, but when the kids were late day after day, I finally went to his class and told him this had to stop. And it did . . . for perhaps a week. When the pattern began again, I started to sense something seriously wrong was going on in his class and decided to play Sherlock Holmes to find out what it was. After asking another teacher to cover the last five minutes of second hour, I lurked outside the industrial arts room to see what I could see.

What I couldn't see were the four boys. Though the room was filled with fourteen-year-olds sanding their doorstops and gluing their cutting boards, my fugitive four were missing in action. When the bell rang to dismiss class, I waited in the hallway as the students filed out, still wondering where my four phantoms might be. About to abandon hope that they were even in the room, I was startled to see them furtively descend a ladder from the upper-level storage area the teacher used to stack the wood that his students would employ in their future projects. I kept my mouth shut the rest of the day but called for bigger guns once the final period ended. Accompanying the assistant principal into the room, we climbed the ladder where we discovered a secret lair that catered to the fantasies of every fourteen-year-old boy. The kids had created a private hideout complete with a battered sofa, back copies of *Playboy*, and a mini-fridge stuffed with Budweiser. Aiding and abetting their behavior in an attempt to be cool, the teacher crossed so many lines they were a tangle of spaghetti, and he was gone by the end of the week.

Because that teacher's behavior was so blatantly offensive, it was easy to dismiss him as an unprofessional outlier who had no business spending even one more second around teenagers. But those well-meaning teachers who invite students into their homes for social visits in the absence of another adult, who revel in the details of much-too-intimate conversations in the privacy of their classroom, or who become Facebook friends to pry into the particulars of their students' personal lives create those gray areas in which it is difficult to know when their concern for their kids becomes a threat to the students and to the school.

In "Teaching 'Outside the Box,'" Dan Coenen captures the essence of the problem and suggests the proper place for teachers to draw the line.

> *Teaching outside the box does not mean partying with students. It certainly does not mean gossiping with them or listening to personal attacks directed at other students or at faculty colleagues. Teaching outside the box does not mean becoming one of the gang or letting it all hang out or abandoning a proper sense of formality and reserve. Students appreciate personal interest, but they also value professional distance. They view it as a sign of respect and a necessary pre-condition for having a productive teacher-student relationship.[3]*

Few teachers go as far as did that misguided colleague I encountered early in my career. But a lot of teachers are like me in that they allow their own need to be liked to create confusion in terms of the teacher-student role. All of the now retired teachers quoted below had to adjust as they figured out how to interact with their students in a professional manner.

> *I look back now and think I wasn't that much older than the students, really. So you try to be more of a buddy to them, you try to be cool. You took it personally when they didn't like your stuff.*

> *When I first started to teach, it was a little awkward because I was twenty-two and some of my students were sixteen, so we weren't that far apart and in some cases they were brothers or sisters of kids I went to school with or of girls I had dated. It was a little weird.*

> *I found myself really wanting the kids to like me, so I would do a lot of things to please the kids, to be cool. Even playing the guitar to some extent. It worked in that I worked it in thematically to some stuff, but I really went overboard to be liked.*

Healthy Relationships = Respect

The key metamorphosis many teachers undergo is to learn to seek their students' respect rather than their friendship. Certainly teachers want their students to like them, and certainly a good relationship with a teacher helps a student to improve. But one teacher who began his career with the hope that his students would see him as their friend shifted his priorities once he matured in his vision of what a teacher should be.

> *I don't really care if my students like me. Most of them do, and that's good, but I want their respect, not their friendship. I think too many teachers—especially young teachers—make that mis-*

take. I want good relationships with my students, but I want to be the adult in the room. I like my students. I consider many of them to be friends, but that's a by-product of what we are doing, not the goal.

What this veteran teacher realizes is that if a teacher's goal is to be liked, then he or she runs the risk of catering to students' desires rather than setting high standards for them that are demanding and difficult. Teaching is a partnership, not a friendship, and though surely all good teachers befriend students throughout their career and keep in touch with them years after graduation, the teacher's role in the partnership is to provide a service to the students that will require sweat and sacrifice on their part. After describing his favorite teacher in "My Teaching Philosophy and the Teachers Who Shaped It," Fred Stephenson concluded his description of him by saying, "Teaching is very much about living an honorable life."[4] Those are words of affection, to be sure, but they are rooted in respect for the man's character and commitment to the success of his students. In fact, Stephenson wrote about that teacher, "What I remember about Dr. Hook was his wisdom, loyalty and dignity. A humble man of greater presence, Dr. Hook was a true gentleman."[5] Again, Stephenson's memories of his onetime mentor are rooted in respect, not a buddy-buddy camaraderie characterized by a too intimate familiarity. Friendship may follow in the wake of respect, but it should be a by-product of a trust that has been earned, not a goal the teacher sets out to achieve. Instead, a teacher's goal in relationships should be to create a classroom climate that is comfortable and safe but that pushes kids to take intellectual chances and strive to get better. That is the reality that one former teacher came to accept.

The best compliment I could ever have from a student is that you really challenged me and forced me to learn and work, but I loved being in that class. That is the ultimate. If you can get those two things—you really feel like you pushed them and you really made them work because those high expectations we sometimes have can have a tendency to make ourselves look good . . . I haven't watered it down.

Students appreciate teachers who make them work as long as that push to succeed is balanced by a dose of genuine concern. Listen to the voices of two graduates of the school where I ended my career reflecting on how relationships and academic prowess are intertwined as they describe their favorite teachers.

> *Her caring mannerisms made the learning environment immensely enjoyable, which fueled people's creative juices to flow. She constantly stretched us to attain the highest level of writing that we could reach and never just doled out an A for kicks. Numerous peers had been so used to A's on everything that they realized they would actually have to work for a good grade. Me too.*

> *Out of all the other teachers I have had, he is one of the few who really respected me and my abilities and treated me as an adult. He managed to mix incredibly high expectations with a high degree of freedom in the classroom and could reconcile his own significant political science knowledge with a recognition of his own limitations. He helped me when I needed help and did not force it on me when it was not necessary. He managed to motivate me, someone without any prior interest in government and a near hatred of history, to work harder than I ever had in a class and to grow to enjoy political science. I learned more and had more fun in his class than in any prior classroom experience to date.*

There is no question that students tend to work harder for a teacher they respect and who they believe cares about them. But it is important to note that researchers have found that a charismatic personality, a sense of comic timing, and the empathy of a village priest are not essential components for a teacher to connect with kids. Ken Bain, the director of the Center for Teaching Excellence at NYU, found through his research focusing on a group of upper-level educators identified as outstanding teachers that one size does not fit all in terms of identifying a teacher's ideal temperament.

Despite some popular beliefs to the contrary, personality played little or no role in successful teaching. We encountered both the bashful and the bold, the restrained and the histrionic. A handful of the subjects played aggressive devil's advocates, avoiding the hostility and the terror to be sure but nevertheless acting quite assertive. Most of them, however, played more subdued and noncombative roles. Some of the teachers treated their students quite formally while others broke down virtually all the conventional social barriers between teacher and learner.[6]

Healthy Relationships = Trust

One of the best teachers with whom I ever worked was a feisty, opinionated genius, a genuine scholar who commanded the classroom through the force of his intellectual expertise and whose sarcastic but good-natured wit kept every student on edge as they wondered who would be the next target of his irrepressible humor. Another great teacher I worked with was a gentle, self-effacing man whose compassion for and investment in his students' welfare was extraordinary and was met by a level of love and respect from them unlike anything I have ever seen. Both teachers were brilliant. Both were beloved. Indeed, though radically different in temperament and approach, each embodied the key component that must develop between students and their teacher for optimal learning to take place—trust. Students who believe that the teacher is invested in their success and will answer repetitive questions patiently, meet with struggling students privately, retest when necessary, and treat them with respect even if they are not doing well in the class are well served by their teacher. Both of these men embraced each of these ideals. The best teachers are not locked into a rigid timetable but will slow down the pace of the class when it becomes apparent that some students are falling behind and will try a variety of strategies to re-explain complex material that goes over the kids' head on the first go-round because of their commitment to the students, not to the sanctity of the curricular agenda.

In a sense, a critical component to building that trust is a sense of humility on the part of a teacher. Remembering his own academic struggles helped one of the retired teachers understand the battles his students faced in the classroom: "I did well in school for the most part, but I always had a hard time in math. So whenever I would get frustrated with the slow kids in my class, I tried to remember what it was like for me as a sixteen-year-old doing everything he could not to look stupid." That same sense of empathy is reflected in the words of a student describing her chemistry teacher, as quoted by Bain in *What the Best College Teachers Do*: "When I heard my professor tell me how much difficulty she first had with chemistry, that gave me the confidence I needed to learn it. I used to think these people were just born with all this knowledge. That's the way a lot of them act."[7] So for a teacher, a sense of perspective, coupled with an ability to view education through the eyes of the kids, is a critical component in building trust in a classroom.

For some teachers, their understanding of the importance of relationships is based upon their own experience in high school. One educator, a man who moved from being a teacher and coach to becoming a principal and later the head of a private school, was an unmotivated student with no real thought of going to college until a high school basketball coach pointed him to a higher vision of what his life could be.

When I was in high school, I started out as not such a great student, not really motivated academically but motivated athletically. . . . I think when I started high school I thought I was going to join the army when I was finished and then go on with life. When I was a sophomore I had a new young coach. . . . I played basketball for him, and he transformed my life. He took an interest in me. He was very tough. He also had that way of connecting and always had the right word to say at the right moment. He would extend himself in a way that built a relationship, and I just loved him. By the time I was a junior, he started pushing me about my future and tried to get me to think about goals and what I wanted to do with my life. He started talking to me about going to college. He started the conversation that got me thinking beyond tomorrow's basketball game and what I was going to do with my life. By the time I was a senior, we were close, and I finally just wanted to be him. I wanted to do with my life exactly what he did with me, where he got to

*know me, built a relationship, challenged me, pushed me, really
expanded my horizons about life. I wanted to teach and coach
but mostly to have an influence on the lives of kids and young
people.*

Another of the retired teachers grew up with a messy home life
and found relationships with his high school basketball coaches to be
both a lifeline and an inspiration for his own career (the names of the
coaches and of the hometown have been changed).

Our home life was so chaotic, and the first time I saw **Chorus
Line***, I thought, "My God, this is a universal story," only I didn't
go to the ballet, I went to the backyard and played basketball for
my escape. So the stability of Terry Ransdorff and Mark Perry
that we didn't have growing up was a big help, and we were
viewed as a successful family in Millersburg. If this is our life,
how many other lives are there like this in Millersburg and the
world that are so messed up? . . . I can go do that and fill that
role in kids' lives and be that, be somebody's Mark Perry. It is
almost a cliché, but I wanted to be somebody's Mark Perry.*

Healthy Relationships = Values

Implicit in both of these accounts is the reality that imparting values is
an important part of what good teachers do. While teachers are hired
to help students learn to speak basic German or balance a ledger in
accounting, most teachers, including these two former teachers, recognize that the influence they have on a student's character is equally vital:

*I've got to know my subject, but I've also got to see it from a
bigger picture. It is not only about writing a paper or commas
or spelling. It is about a bigger picture of how this helps you be
a better human being. No matter what school you're at, you
are helping them learn of those characteristics that are lifelong
skills and helping them hone what is being taught—or maybe
isn't being taught—in other places. There are a certain number
of those character traits that if we don't do that, because of who*

we are and how we relate to kids, they can be just as important in many regards as the discipline we are teaching. One doesn't take the place of the other, but those two things to me are the non-negotiables. That's what every good teacher does.

There is that connection between the teacher and student that gives the teacher an opportunity to truly have an impact on the thinking, on the character, on the goals, on the dreams of the student. I think the ability to do that is transformative when it comes to making a difference in the lives of kids. And that ability—in so many ways it is a gift—to develop a relationship that is built on affection, trust, respect, honesty. If a teacher has that, that teacher can really make a difference.

I never realized just how much attention kids pay to the investment teachers make in their lives until the final days of my son Jeff's high school years. When our school's girls' soccer team advanced to the state quarterfinals, Jeff and two of his friends joined me for the long ride to a faraway field for the match. When the game ended and we began the drive home, one of Jeff's friends remarked how thoughtful it was that one of his teachers and his wife had driven all the way to the game because he knew the couple's children were still toddlers, and their nights out were infrequent. The other friend, a starting guard on the basketball team, then commented that he always noticed which teachers attended his games, and that observation led to a twenty-minute dissection of which teachers came to what events at the school—who was into the theater, who was into football, who was into the instrumental music concerts, and who never came to any student events at all. These three senior boys—none of them models of sensitivity—were so aware of who gave their time to support student events outside of school hours that for the duration of the trip home they literally worked their way down the hallway from classroom to classroom naming each teacher in turn and acknowledging those teachers who seemed most interested in cheering on their students. That drive provided me with an unforgettable lesson of the importance of investing in the lives and interests of students. If I wanted to show a student I cared, then I needed to show up.

Not every teacher shares that point of view. Early in my career, our football team went on a miraculous winning streak after years of mediocrity. Though we had won only three games the year before, during this dream season the team suddenly got hot, rolled to the district championship, and then upset one of the area's perennial powers in an unexpected display of quick-strike football to set up a quarterfinal match with our archrivals. Because winning was so unexpected and so new for the students, the halls were abuzz, and all the kids wanted to talk about on the day of the game was the opportunity to go to State if we could only best the very team that had spanked us for years. As I was leaving the building at the end of the day, I asked one of the veteran teachers if he was going to that night's big game. I will never forget his response: "When you have been teaching as long as I have, there is no such thing as a big game."

I get it. He was right that high school football really isn't all that important, and he was right that way too much importance is attached to sports in high schools across America. But to the kids playing the game this *was* a big deal, and to the other kids caught up in the euphoria attached to winning, the game provided an outlet for innocent energy and an opportunity to build memories of a night with their friends filled with promise and excitement. Teachers don't have to buy in to the nonsense that can come with high school athletics, but they should buy into caring about what the kids care about, and if that means showing up at a sporting event or concert or play as a way of establishing a bond of concern, that is a trust earned at little cost.

Healthy Relationships = Love

While it is self-evident that a strong trust between student and teacher might well foster personal growth in a teenager, it is less obvious that such a bond would have any impact on a student's academic progress, but that is the argument Cheryl Blau makes in "The Magical Teacher" in arguing that the relationships a teacher has with his or her students are far more important in facilitating learning than any other factor, including whatever specific pedagogical or curricular approaches a teacher might adopt.[8] H. A. Dawe echoes that idea when he writes about the way students come to embrace knowledge: "We learned to prize certain ideas because we admired the individuals who presented them."[9] That principle ought to be self-evident, according to Howard Hendricks in *Teaching to Change Lives*.

> *All learning begins at the feeling level. People accept what they feel disposed to accept, and they reject what they feel disposed to reject. If their attitude is positive, they tend to embrace what they hear. If their attitude is negative, they tend to walk away from it. If I have negative feelings about you, I will reject what you're saying because I reject you. But if I like you—and I know you're interested in me—you can get me to do the most incredible things in all the world.*[10]

To a person, the retired teachers I interviewed agreed with this thinking. In identifying what they perceived to be the non-negotiables required for a successful classroom career, all but one began by saying that loving kids was absolutely essential, and the one who did not begin there mentioned that factor quickly. An often-heard adage used in youth ministry is that a youth worker must "win the right to be heard." Though teachers have a captive audience that a youth pastor does not, most teachers would agree with that principle, as these three teachers suggest.

> *You have to know the students very, very well. I don't think I would be well suited to teaching in an environment where the desks were in rows and I didn't know the kids as people insofar as what sports they played and what hobbies they have. In order to motivate them, I need to know them as people and I need to know them as learners. I need to know how to tap into their learning style. What are their strengths? What are their weaknesses? What skills do they have when they come to me? So we pretty much spend the first quarter of the year getting to know all that, so I get comfortable long about the second quarter because I don't feel you can be effective with young people if you don't meet them where they are.*

> *I am convinced that the essence of good teaching is the relationship between students and teacher, so I really try to develop*

a relationship with each of my students or what I try to teach them will be meaningless—just a bunch of words.

Early in my career I was so focused on learning the content and how to present the content that I kind of lost sight of the idea that we are not teaching content, we are teaching people. Once you remember that, it all works. Really, how much content do they really need out of my class? Not that much . . . maybe 10 percent. It's the relationships you build that matter most.

For many of these teachers, their thinking was influenced by becoming a father or mother and learning to see the world of the classroom through the eyes of a parent with a newfound sense of compassion for their students.

What I wanted for my own children was somebody to take care of them, somebody to help them be smart. For the last twenty years I realized kids don't come to class to learn the material, they come to learn you and the material will come along for the ride. If they don't connect with you, if they think you don't care about them, you can have the best lesson plan in the world, and it will have no impact on that kid. I began to see that if you pay attention to kids and understanding I want to treat this kid the way I want teachers to treat my daughters, how can I possibly become callous or ignore this kid, because if he is mine I want the teacher to care for this kid.

I think part of [becoming a good teacher] was having David as a child because David was an unmotivated student, and he is not a great reader, and so I think that when I thought about how David was going to be taught and how I would have taught him early in my career, I realized I would have just dismissed him or ignored him. I wouldn't have been mean to him, but he would have faded into the background. I began to teach to the Davids in my class.

For Melanie, it didn't matter so much what the course was, it mattered who the teacher was. If she had a good relationship with the teacher, she did better. If she hated the teacher, she did worse. It didn't matter what the subject was. I learned from that. It really has more to do with relationships than it does to do with content or anything like that.

The truth is that most teachers—at least the good ones—are idealists. Almost everyone has suffered through the class of a man or woman who is marking time until retirement, reading from the same notes he or she compiled years before, but the best teachers are those who see their task as a combination of skill and information transfer plus character formation, and who bring great passion to the classroom because of their commitment to their students' minds *and* hearts. No teacher can possibly connect with every student, but every teacher connects with some, and that interplay is one of the great blessings of the profession. While recognizing their limits, the best teachers do what they can to make a difference, as one retired teacher recalls in reflecting on his own experience:

You want to save everybody but it is hopeless. But it is kind of like the old cartoon where the little boy is throwing starfish in the ocean and the old man asks, "What are you doing?"
  "I'm throwing back the starfish that have washed up."
  "You can't save all these starfish."
  "But I can save this one."

The rewards of building relationships with kids are endless, and most teachers would surely say that it is those relationships that they treasure more than a tightly constructed lesson plan on the Treaty of Paris. Teachers rarely know the influence they have since few kids take the time to say thank you when the school year ends, and even fewer take the time to write a note of appreciation. But on rare occasions students whose lives have been touched will draw back the curtain to allow a teacher to see just how much he or she has meant to them. On the last day of his long career, one teacher had one of those moments of bliss that he will remember all his life.

One of the most glorious moments of my life was my last day, my last class . . . I even took a picture of the classroom when I was ready to leave. I was a little disappointed that none of the kids had said, "It's been great, good luck to you." I was just ready to leave when one of my students knocked on the door and said, "Can I see you for a second?" She came in and started telling me good luck and then two more and then four more, and by the end there were fifty kids in a circle. She had put together a book. She had contacted some of my students from twenty to twenty-five years ago. She had letters, pictures. When I talk to new teachers, I tell them you are going to have really crappy days, but you are going to have glorious days like that that you will feast on forever when you realize that the kids do love you and you love them. People who say don't smile until Christmas and don't get too close to the kids? That's crap. You need to love those kids, and they need to love you.

Teachers don't teach for or expect those all too rare moments. But when they occur, the hours of grading, phone calls from angry parents, and disengaged students vanish in a fog of forgetfulness forever. That's when teachers realize that they have indeed created an unbreakable bond that will impact the world into the next generation. That's when teachers realize that they have lived a life that really matters.

Reflections

1. What are students afraid of in your class? How might you be contributing to their fear? What steps can you take to make your class a place in which they feel free to test their ideas and take chances without fear of ridicule?
2. How do you ensure that you maintain a professional relationship with your students? How would you define a healthy teacher-student relationship?
3. Fred Stephenson says that "Teaching is very much about living an honorable life." What would "living an honorable life" before your students look like for you?
4. Who were the teachers who inspired you or encouraged you in your adolescence? How did they do that?

Action Items

1. Which teachers in your school seem to connect best with students while still maintaining a healthy professional distance? Talk to each of them, exploring how they achieve a sense of trust with their students without imposing on the kids' private lives.

2. What values do you hope to communicate to your students? Do your lessons, do your assessments, do your interactions with your students reflect those values?

Understanding Classroom Management

It is obvious that issues of classroom control are the ultimate bugaboo for many first-year teachers. Managing to keep kids quiet, corralling them in their seats, keeping them on task, and getting them to treat each other with respect can pose the ultimate trial, one that drives many teachers to throw up their hands in total panic and fight the urge to sprint screaming to the principal's office to quit. Though most of the disturbances teachers face are minor, it is hard to go too many years without running into major issues that reach far beyond the ability of most teachers to handle. I was welcomed to the world of student teaching when, on my first day in the school, two boys blocked the stairway to the second floor by spraying every student who attempted to pass with a blast of Mace. A student at my next school was a junior-grade pyromaniac who regularly asked for a pass to the bathroom so he could set the trash can on fire, causing the sprinkler system to kick in and the school to be evacuated at least once a month. Years later, a student I had never seen before bombarded me with a remarkable fusillade of profanity unprecedented in its volume, duration, and creativity when I tried to chase him out of the hallway so he could take a final exam he had chosen to skip. He was so loud and so original in his pairings of the more colorful phrases in our language that teachers all along the hallway left their classes to stand in slack-jawed amazement as they listened to his obscene display of linguistic virtuosity. And in the most stunning display of chutzpah I ever witnessed, an honors student robbed a bank on his way to school and then showed up as scheduled to take his English final. *And* he got an A.

Like most young teachers, I struggled with classroom management issues in the early years of my career. My classes in year one were too often anarchic, in year two were balanced on the razor thin line between control and chaos most days, and in year three were reasonably calm. It took me a while to find the sweet spot between friendliness and firmness. In fact, it was not until I began to think less about what I was doing to promote order in the classroom and more about the inner lives of my students that I began to solve the problems of control I had struggled to master for too long.

While I can appreciate the brilliance of the paintings of Caravaggio or Van Gogh, while I know that the operas of Mozart or Verdi are sublime, at my core I am a philistine, the kind of man real art aficionados look at with utter disdain. I am a man of the Midwest, a man with meat and potato tastes who thinks the Austin Powers movies are high comedy and the Zac Brown Band exemplifies all that is right about music. So it should come as no surprise that the painting *The Girl at the Mirror* by Norman Rockwell is one of

Girl at Mirror, by Norman Rockwell. Printed by permission of the Norman Rockwell Family Agency. Copyright © 1954 the Norman Rockwell Family Entities.

my favorites. Rockwell may not have the skills or the cachet of someone like Caravaggio or Van Gogh, but this painting touches me deeply. As the father of one girl, as the grandfather of another, and as the teacher of hundreds and hundreds more, I look at this painting with a sense of sadness every time I see it. This young girl sits gazing at her image that, in her mind, does not measure up. She will never be as beautiful as the actress in the photo, will never be the idealized beauty she would like to be. She carries a self-portrait in her head that says she is not good enough, that she is a failure because the standards Hollywood has set are so high that she will be burdened by her ordinariness until the day she dies. What breaks my heart is that every student who ever walked into my classroom carried a similar picture of themselves in their own head. None of them thought they measured up. All of them determined their own place in the classroom pecking order by gauging themselves against their peers, and too many found themselves wanting.

Knowing the Kids

For most kids in middle school and high school, adolescence is a period of enormous insecurity, a time during which many are haunted by their sense that somehow everyone else seems to have it all together, but they do not. That, coupled with the unhappy reality that too many students walk into class each day carrying the burden of a miserable home life, creates a scenario rife with the possibility that something can go seriously wrong. Kids who are abused, neglected, ignored, or caught in the middle of a domestic battleground can become powder kegs of insecurity and anger with sometimes troubling results. Those emotions manifest themselves in many ways. Some kids become withdrawn, doing everything they can to become invisible so that those around them will not discern their self-perceived inadequacies or dreary circumstances at home. Some rebel, lashing out in anger because no one seems to care, and no one seems willing to help lift them out of despair. Some preen for attention, hoping that the laughter and applause of their classmates will validate their sense of self. Whatever the experience of the students' personal lives, the truth is that because all of them bring their own reality into the classroom, the potential for disruption always exists. Unless teachers are keenly aware of the interpersonal dynamics going on in the lives of their students, they may well miss the clues that can quickly tip a class into disorder. One now retired teacher, who was assisted by a teacher's aide each day, describes how she made a point of making eye contact with each of her students as they came to class as a way to assess what issues they might be facing and head off potential problems.

When they came into the door, they shook hands every day with one of us. . . . That gave us the opportunity to look into their eyes, to make eye contact, and it might be for the last time all day, one on one. It gave us a chance to see if we saw anything going wrong right now. You knew if you saw someone walking in with bloodshot eyes, with a puffy face or with their head down so they wouldn't look at you it's a pretty good signal. How many times do we really look at that? It helped prevent a lot of problems and headed off immediate things that could have gone wrong. It's funny, but when you help them to address their needs, then they are more likely to be with you when it is time to buckle down.

That sensitivity to what is going on in a student's life is one way to curtail trouble, but more importantly, it is a way to discern whatever issues might be affecting a student's performance and behavior in the classroom so that a teacher can both empathize and address them if possible. A former teacher recalls what she learned through the example of a young man who fell asleep every day in her class. No matter what she did, she could not keep him awake and left most days frustrated with him because of his disrespect and inattention. One day, however, she substituted for another teacher and saw the same behavior from the same student in that classroom as well. Now doubly upset, she warned him that he would never graduate if he failed each of these classes because of his drowsiness. His response stunned her. Telling her that he provided the sole support for his brothers and sisters, he explained that he worked the night shift all week and, despite his desire to finish his education, was too exhausted to remain awake during class. That encounter changed the way this teacher viewed her students from that point on.

That put a whole different face to what had been happening in class. It started me thinking a whole lot more about the entire student and what he had gone through and what he brings into the classroom every day. So over the years I don't think I have lowered my standards, but I do think I have become a lot more flexible.

The first step in reducing conflict in the classroom, then, is simply to know the students well. The point that relationships matter has already been made, but understanding who wants to be left alone, who needs encouragement, who likes to be the center of attention, and who is facing serious problems at home is one element in structuring a classroom environment that is safe for everyone and in which productive learning can take place.

Knowing the students well forestalls problems on another level too. Kids simply behave better in classes in which they respect their teacher, and teachers in tune with the academic and social needs of their students can tailor the tone and the pace of their classrooms to accommodate those needs. A teacher who is sensitive to the ups and downs of a student's life or a class's frame of mind and who has the flexibility to adapt his or her demands accordingly can earn a great deal of relational capital simply by treating his students with compassion. The principle is really simple—when kids like and respect their teacher, they are less likely to disrupt what is going on. One retired teacher reflects on how she dealt with the emotional roller coaster of her students' moods in an effort to keep them on her side.

> *I kind of liked to think of myself as an artist in the sense that I knew when to use the fine brushes and I knew when to get out the paintbrush and swat. I knew when the class needed a gentle stroke and when it needed a heavy lather. I seemed to understand that pretty well.*

We're All in This Together

Another element that helps to offset problems between students and their teacher is the latter's ability to communicate that he or she is in the battle *with* the kids, that their teacher has their back. Kids mess up. They forget their textbook, speak out of turn, talk trash, lose their temper, and neglect to do their homework. Every one of those situations is an annoyance. Every one of them means the teacher has to decide whether to drop the hammer or extend an olive branch. And though dropping the hammer is sometimes the only option, at times the better choice is to extend a degree of grace, as this longtime teacher points out.

> *Grace is better than rules. Every kid needs grace; every kid needs mercy more than they need somebody that is nitpicky about everything. I don't care if a kid has everything going for him or her, they still need mercy, they still need grace, they still need somebody who is going to say, "You need a break today." That's what I want for my own kids. As a parent, I want a teacher who cares about them and cares that they had a bad night the night before. I don't want a teacher for my kids who is just going to say, "I don't care what your life is like. You still have to do this or that." . . . Across the board kids need teachers who care about them and are willing to bend the rules when it is necessary.*

One of the retired teachers learned the value of grace in a most embarrassing way following a basketball game in which his team blew a big lead late in the fourth quarter only to lose at the buzzer. Frustrated by his players' inability to handle the pressure of a close game, he blasted them following the loss, ripping them for their gutlessness and sloppiness at full volume. Satisfied that he had delivered a stirring motivational tirade, he walked out of his locker room only to bump into John Wooden, the legendary UCLA basketball coach famous for treating his players gently. With a knowing look, Wooden simply asked one question: "What did you just teach those kids?" As the teacher recalls, "I felt pretty small. You can't say much to John Wooden." That night marked a turning point in this coach's career. Going forward, he did his best to remember that his players were seventeen-year-olds who needed a word of encouragement, not NBA superstars who needed a kick in the butt. Whether in the classroom or on the court, teachers need a dose of perspective to ensure that kids know their teacher is on their side.

None of that can occur unless a teacher knows his or her students well and can sense when it is time to ease up and when it is appropriate to ratchet up the pressure. So one way to combat classroom control issues is to be in tune with what is going on in the lives of the kids and in the class as a whole.

Setting the Rules of the Road

Another way to combat classroom control issues is to define one's standards clearly so that students know what is expected of them. Kids need to understand what the teacher requires, and unless a teacher articulates what he demands up front, how are students supposed to know what rules really matter to that teacher? With that in mind, during the first week of school I always passed out a handout I called "The Law of the Land," a sheet that detailed my expectations concerning due dates, late work, food in the classroom, cell phone use, missed assignments, and other procedural issues. That way students knew that the standards I would enforce were neither arbitrary nor directed at any individual who violated one of these edicts. When a student crossed a line, I did not have to make up a policy on the spot because by determining and communicating what I believed and expected, the kids knew the rules of the game beforehand. The decision to define my guidelines in advance was inspired by one of the principals for whom I worked who stressed four key ideas that steered his approach to establishing parameters for his students when he was still a classroom teacher.

- Tell them what game we are playing.
- Tell them the rules.
- Tell them how we keep score.
- Tell them when the game is over.

When I first began teaching, I had little idea of the importance of building classroom structures to simplify the flow of a class and to cut down on the opportunities for disorder, so when it came time to turn in assignments or to divide the class into small groups, I had no idea how to do either efficiently. But as the four guidelines above suggest, kids need to know what is expected of them and what will happen if they do not acquiesce so that they can operate within the teacher's tolerance level for disruption.

In observing other teachers over the years, one truth became apparent: the younger the students, the more important it is that the teacher establish a clearly understood set of procedures and policies to direct the many movements that occur within a single hour of class.

Because I taught only twelfth grade during my last dozen years as a teacher, I gave relatively little thought to the need to define the basic domestic chores that make up a class period and so focused only on larger issues in "The Law of the Land." Seniors, for the most part, are mature enough to handle transitions and resent a bunch of procedures they regard as petty. But without those procedures in place, a seventh-grade class can descend into chaos in an instant. When I sat through back-to-back lessons of one of our finest seventh-grade teachers, I was impressed that she had clearly thought through and communicated her answers to each of these questions.

- How will I get the kids' attention to signal the start of class or a transition to a new activity?
- How will I call on students when I want them to answer questions?
- How will I structure our use of time during independent work?
- What are my expectations for group work? Can kids sit on the floor? Can they sit on the tables? Can they go in the Commons area outside of the classroom to do their work?
- Will I allow kids to bring drinks into the classroom? Food?
- What will I ask kids to do if they finish their seatwork early?
- What procedures should kids follow in turning in assignments?
- Can students listen to their iPods with earphones when they are doing individual work?
- How will I distribute materials to the class?
- How will I return work to the students?
- How will we transition to a lab?
- How will I begin the day to ensure the kids are on task immediately?
- When we are using technology, how will we pass out and collect laptops efficiently?
- When, if ever, can students have their cell phones out of their backpacks? Their iPads?
- What does it mean to be tardy?
- How will we wrap up the day?

- What are the procedures for going to the bathroom? To get a drink? To sharpen a pencil? To go to their locker?

Those kinds of questions might seem excessive to someone who has never experienced life in a classroom, but as one who began his career as a middle school teacher, I wish someone had walked me through a list like this before I ever began my career. Because I had not thought enough about issues like these, I had to respond on the fly when disorder threatened to engulf the classroom, and my answers were more than haphazard because of it. Defining and communicating the guidelines a teacher expects can cut down on the kind of chaos I had to learn to overcome after the fact.

But doing so does not solve the problem. No matter how carefully teachers define their expectations, no matter how thoughtfully they build relationships with their students, no matter how willing they are to extend grace when they see a student's misbehavior is fueled by circumstances beyond his or her control, sometimes the class blows up anyway. And when that happens, good teachers really earn their pay because a disciplinary crisis poorly handled can irrevocably rupture the relationship with a student and make it impossible ever to reach him or her again. One of the retired teachers, a man noted for his rapport with his students, said that his biggest regret in all his years in education was the day he literally climbed over a table to manhandle a student who had cussed him out. My biggest regret is similar. Years ago I lost my temper with a senior girl who had driven me to my breaking point and angrily dragged her out of my classroom in front of her peers. Though each of these events happened more than two decades ago, both of us remain ashamed that we let our emotions overrule our good sense and our duty to treat our students well.

Though the freedom to impose disciplinary actions that would today seem objectionable was open to teachers in the 1960s and '70s—we were, for instance, encouraged to paddle misbehaving students at the first school in which I taught—in retrospect some of what we were allowed to do was indefensible. For one of the former teachers, her treatment of a difficult student haunted her for years and led to a serious reevaluation of how she would deal with trouble in the future.

I had a kid named Steve. I was fresh out of school—he wasn't being a bad kid, but he was just being obnoxious. I remember one time him getting in trouble and telling him, "Lie down and put your nose on the floor." He did it, but I remember he stood up and he walked out and he said, "I did that for you this time, but I will never do that again.". . . He was absolutely right. I was totally and completely wrong. Twenty-five years later when I read of his appointment as a youth pastor, I wrote him a letter as my way of saying that there is a teacher out there who is somewhat competent, and you dramatically affected the way I deal with my students.

There are better ways to deal with disruptive adolescents. Though every situation is unique and every teacher has to find his own disciplinary style, teachers need to keep a few key principles in mind in discerning how to keep the lid on when the kettle is about to blow.

Don't Take Misbehavior Personally

In my deluded self-importance, I dramatically overestimated the time my students spent thinking about me when I was a young teacher. Grossly misreading their misbehavior, I worried that every act of defiance was a direct attack on my authority. As a result, I needlessly escalated minor skirmishes into full-fledged battles because I thought their misconduct was pointed at me. The truth is that I was a blip in their lives, an irritant at best, someone who happened to be standing in the way of their need for attention or their anger fueled by something wholly apart from the classroom. I may have supplied the fuse to ignite an explosion, but the root cause of that explosion was usually based upon factors far beyond my understanding. Only when I began to realize that a student's disobedience had little to do with anything I had done or who I was did I begin to take their mischief in stride. One of the retired teachers learned the same lesson.

I think you might take personally things kids might do or say as a beginning teacher. You might tend to be very hurt or very angry, but you learn over the years which things to let roll—this too shall pass—and when you are going to take a stand and say, "That is unacceptable."

Only rarely was a student mad at me when he or she acted out. By dealing with the offense itself rather than treating it as if it were a personal affront, I was able to make the misbehavior the issue and not threaten the relationship between us. That meant doing everything I could to ensure that emotion played little part in dealing with the incident so that once it was past us, we could go on as if it had never happened at all, a point worth exploring a bit more below.

Keep the Emotion Out of It

In an ideal world, when it is time to lower the boom on a student who will not cooperate, teachers would seek to emulate Mr. Spock from *Star Trek* and channel the emotion-free Vulcan side of their nature. But that's impossible. Some students know how to trigger an eruption from their teachers and love to provoke a scene by appealing to their weak spot over and over and over. Even teachers with the patience of St. Francis reach a point where they just can't take it anymore. First comes mild annoyance, then mounting irritation, then escalating frustration, and finally the explosion of anger that sets the class afire. So let's concede that no one will handle discipline issues perfectly. All teachers have those moments they regret, those moments they said or did something that they wish they could take back and pray they never repeat.

To combat the problem, it helps to clearly define the endgame in handling classroom outbreaks. I have been driven by a wide range of largely self-serving aims in facing down students who simply would not comply. At times I have been motivated by a drive to assert my authority, to use power as a club to bully a student into line. So I would get in a student's face, going all Clint Eastwood on him in a mano a mano duel of testosterone. At times I have sought revenge, seeking to embarrass a student who had embarrassed me in front of the class. At times my goal was to avoid losing face, so I would call out a student in front of her peers in an attempt to make clear who was in charge. Each of these responses was a reflection of my own immaturity, a sign that I was no Mr. Spock but an idiot who cared more about his own ego than the welfare of his students.

As I see it, there are really only two acceptable goals in a typical disciplinary situation—stopping the behavior and maintaining the relationship with the student. Let's not pull punches. Kids can screw up big time, and when a situation turns violent or threatens the safety of other students, a teacher must intervene forcefully and immediately to protect those caught up in the situation. But most discipline issues that arise in school fall far short of that mark. For the mundane acts of disobedience—excessive talking, disrespectful comments directed at the teacher or other students, refusing to take a seat—teachers need to respond firmly and promptly by confronting the student in a low key but persuasive manner.

When my students got out of line, my go-to move was to walk to the student's desk, put my hand on the back of his chair, lean down, make eye contact, and say firmly, "You are *not* going to do this again. Is that understood?" Then I walked away so that the student did not have an opportunity to say anything that would escalate the situation. There was no drama, there was no rancor, there was nothing more than an emphatic expression of what I expected. Ninety percent of the time that is all it took to end the situation. Other times I would use humor. If I lost the entire class, if the students all became distracted and chattered away as if I were not even there, I would say in a cheery voice, "Excuse me, did I just become the Invisible Man?" or "I must have made a mistake. I thought this was a classroom, not a pep rally." That's not exactly material worthy of Louis CK, but it made the point without having to raise my voice and brought matters under control without provoking a confrontation. A former high school teacher who now teaches on the university level recalls the way he used humor to get his students' attention: "One of my old favorites (and it only worked once for any class) when the kids were ignoring me was to say in a loud voice 'SEX.' They would immediately freeze and look my way. I would then quietly continue 'is not the topic for today, but now that I have your attention, we can move on to'. . . ."

During my last year of teaching, I had a class in which the only four boys in it were all good friends, and at least twice a week they would begin to regale each other with their favorite in-jokes and memories of the previous weekend as if the rest of us were not even there. My standard response to their outbreaks was to grab a chair, sit down next to them, and invite them to let us all in on the exchange. That brought their conversation to a halt most days, and because the dialogue was always good-natured, we were able to get back to business quickly. The truth is that most kids are more than willing to work with teachers who defuse a situation with humor or submit to their authority when teachers deal with disobedience with a non-threatening but firm hand. Teddy Roosevelt's old maxim "Speak softly but carry a big stick" may have been a statement reflecting his approach to diplomacy, but it is not a bad place to start in dealing with disciplinary issues either.

De-escalation Is Your Responsibility

When things go really bad and tempers flare, someone has to be the adult in the room—and it had better be the one who really is the adult. For a teacher to lose his temper in the face of a student's misconduct is a mistake that may take weeks to overcome. When I dragged the young woman into the hallway that day, I lost the rest of the class for the remainder of the year. Though that incident occurred late in the semester, and though to that point I had a good relationship with that group of students, in the three weeks remaining I never was able to reestablish genuine rapport with the kids who had witnessed my anger firsthand. I had violated their trust, and though they were gracious and continued to cooperate till the end, the mood of the room shifted that day, a fault that was entirely mine. Losing my temper was a terrible mistake, and the ripples caused by that incident never fully subsided.

A second incident a few years later taught me another lesson about de-escalation. On a cold March morning a few days before spring break, a normally even-keeled, good-natured senior stormed into my third-hour class obviously upset over something that had just happened. As he sat in his desk just before the bell rang, he quietly muttered an especially pointed profanity referring to his second-hour teacher because he thought she had treated him unfairly. Though only a few students heard him say it, they reacted in shock because his anger was so intense. I knew I could not let this go. To ignore his remark would have been an act of disrespect toward a colleague and would have sent a terrible message to the young man and to his classmates that it was okay to so blatantly blast a teacher. But this student was seething, and I sensed immediately that to call him out would have risked an explosion that he would later regret and I did not want to incite. So I said very firmly that his words were unacceptable and that I would see him in the hallway immediately after class.

That sent a clear message to him and to those who had heard his words that his remark was out of line and that I would deal with it directly. Should I have sent him to the office immediately? Maybe. But by giving the young man some time to calm down, we avoided a con-frontation that would surely have been contentious and might have caused him to further intensify the offense. By the time class was over, he made a beeline to my desk to apologize, insisted he would go at once to the other teacher's room to tell her he was sorry, and offered to ask my third-hour class for forgiveness since he knew he had crossed an uncrossable line.

This was a really good kid, a young man who worked hard, almost always made sound decisions, and said something he absolutely should not have said. What he did was wrong, and I had to address his action. But by giving him some time to decompress, he responded exactly as he should have. He came to terms with his mistake, owned it, and agreed to step up and take responsibility. Had I chosen to call him out at once, matters could have turned ugly, so ugly that his anger may have erupted and turned an unfortunate incident into a nasty battle that may have scarred our relationship for the rest of the year and increased his offense exponentially. Teachers need to treat blatant misbehavior seriously, but sometimes it is best to step back from the emotion of the moment and let the feelings cool before deciding what to do. As one of the retired teachers says, "I know I am going to win the war at the end, and I don't worry about the battles as much as I used to." Kids need some space when they are riled up beyond reason, and a cooling off period can keep a volcano of emotions in check.

Another step teachers may need to take to de-escalate tensions is to apologize when they are the ones who have blown their cool. Though the number of times I lost my temper or treated a student badly was thankfully small, I did it enough to spend more time than I would have liked telling a student or a class that I was sorry. Without exception the apology was well received and in almost every case made the relationship even stronger. After I apologized to a senior girl for an incident that took place in class, she wrote me a note at the end of the year that included this message: "Your apology to me regarding the small group situation was something that most others would not do in that situation. I so appreciate your sensitivity to the feelings of others and your willingness to humble yourself." Notes like that serve as a reminder that teachers should step up to face the music more, not less.

A Sense of Humor Goes a Long Way

I stepped into our dean of students' office one day after school to leave him a note when I saw a disciplinary form sitting on his desk awaiting his action. A teacher had driven into the school parking lot that morning, and his car had been bombarded with a barrage of snowballs from a group of junior boys hiding in the bushes. Enraged, he had written to the administrator asking him to discipline the kids for their disrespectful assault, insisting that they be sent to after-school suspension. Those same boys had bombed my car that same morning as I entered the parking lot only moments before my colleague, and I had shaken my fist in mock fury as I drove on, promptly forgetting about what they had done as soon as I got out of my car. To me—and to all the other teachers whose cars were most certainly hit—the snowball onslaught was nothing more than an attempt to have some fun. But for one teacher it was an occasion for outrage and a reason to bring a group of boys before the judgment seat.

Teachers have to decide what to let go and what to deal with. If a student deliberately defies a teacher or insults a fellow student, then the hammer must fall. But when kids are simply being kids, when they are trying to relieve the monotony of a lengthy, sometimes boring school year with an act of harmless mischief, then at times the better choice is to look the other way and even laugh along.

Here is a perfect example. Since for much of my career my classes were discussion based, I arranged the tables in the classroom in a square and every day moved to a different spot so that I always sat by different students. A few years ago a handful of students became obsessed with trying to smuggle a plastic fork into my pants pocket every time they sat next to me, hoping that at some point in the period I would reach into my pocket to retrieve a pen and would discover their handiwork. Every time they succeeded I would roar in mock outrage, and this prank became one of the running jokes of the year. Was it a violation of my personal space? I guess so. Was it an attack upon my dignity? Someone might think so, but the kids thought the prank was hilarious (so did I), and the game of cat-and-mouse we played for the rest of the year was fun for everyone. Why turn a moment of shared goodwill into a battleground? A teacher's ability to laugh at himself can create a comfortable atmosphere for the kids, and teachers who can accept being the butt of a good-natured joke can help break up the tedium of a long, long school year. Teaching is certainly serious, but teachers don't always have to be.

Consistency Matters . . . Except When It Doesn't

Most authorities on classroom control strongly stress the need to enforce rules consistently, and I agree . . . to a point. Though I rarely wanted to draw a line in the sand, when I did, I had to act when someone crossed it. One of the items in "The Law of the Land" was that if I caught a student doing homework for another teacher during my class, I would throw that homework out the window since I expected kids to actually focus on English when they were *in* English. Though a monsoon might be raging outside, I would toss the essay or worksheet for another class into the storm. I only had to do it once or twice each year before the word got out; as soon as the kids saw I was serious, that was the end of the problem. On those occasions when I created a rule and then let it slide because I wanted to be a nice guy or did not have the energy to combat the offense, however, the odds that forbidden behavior would escalate were astronomical. So consistency did make a difference.

But as Ralph Waldo Emerson famously said, "A foolish consistency is the hobgoblin of little minds." That's why it is wise to limit the number of issues that really matter so that a teacher does not spend the entire year drawing lines students are tempted to cross and fighting battles that are not worth winning. Those few concerns that mean the most to a teacher may be sacrosanct, but flexibility is a teacher's ally when it comes to much of what goes on in a classroom. Define the policies that matter, communicate them, and enforce them. But part of maturing as a teacher is deciding what is essential and what is not because creating needless barriers between a teacher and the students can only lead to conflict. A teacher can regulate the flow of a classroom with a system of procedures that kids are to follow (like the ones I established in "The Law of the Land"), but classroom *rules* mandating behavior should be simple and obvious. Teachers who hold their authority loosely establish a classroom environment in which the students have a fair degree of freedom, all within the teacher's tolerance for what is acceptable behavior and what is not. Here is the atmosphere one now retired teacher tried to create as he evolved in his thinking about classroom management:

> *You do a much better job of deciding which issues, which challenges are worth making a stand for and which ones are better addressed with discretion. You know . . . some things you have to take the time and energy to focus on and other things you are going to have to say we are going to let these things slide—they are not that important. We are going to focus on what really matters. So you learn to make subjective evaluations of what is truly important more effectively.*

Based upon that philosophy, this teacher defined his essentials, communicated them up front, and dealt with their violation when the students failed to comply. Consistency matters, but so does a teacher's judgment, and knowing when to draw the lines and when to resist the temptation to do so can help create a classroom environment that is comfortable for teacher and students alike. As one former teacher suggests, that stance benefits all parties in that as a teacher becomes more patient in the face of a disruptive student, that example sets the tone for the entire classroom and communicates the way the conflict should be handled. Like parents, teachers need to pick their battles, so creating a list of rules that really matter can set the tone for a class in which students can thrive, and the teacher does not have to spend his day putting out fires that never should have ignited.

Here is one fire that didn't need to ignite. Many years ago one of my students came to class incensed that his history teacher in the previous period had just assigned forty pages of reading and a three-page essay reflecting on that reading to be turned in the next day. While that is a lot of work for one evening under any circumstances, the fact that the St. Louis Cardinals were playing in game seven of the National League Championship series for the right to go to the World Series that same night infuriated this student, as well as most of his classmates, because the teacher seemed oblivious to the students' interest in the game. Loving the Cardinals is a civic duty in St. Louis, and risking the students' goodwill because the teacher was new to the school and the city was a bad idea. I went to her and suggested she move the deadline back a day; doing so would have little effect on her curricular timetable and would send the right message to the kids. When she did so and word began to spread throughout the school, no one accused her of being weak because she had changed her mind. Instead, many of her students rushed to thank her, and her flexibility earned her a lot of points from the baseball fans in her class. The lesson is simple: Draw the lines when they matter. When they don't, keep an open mind.

One caveat about the need for flexibility must be mentioned. Effective discipline is a school-wide affair, and teachers who ignore building policies they don't like undermine the efforts of both their colleagues in the classroom and the administration to maintain the academic atmosphere that has been set by those in charge. If the school does not allow students to eat in class and a teacher turns the classroom into a junior-grade dining hall, he or she has effectively undercut every teacher who is trying to enforce the standard. If the administration bans cell phone use in class and a teacher converts the room into a miniature AT&T call center, his or her decision to circumvent the rule makes it that much harder for the rest of the faculty to maintain the policy. Flexibility has its place, but it also has its limits.

Confidence Makes a Difference

Students read their teachers' moods, of course. Like sharks, kids have a nose for blood in the water, and those with a disposition to misbehave see new teachers as fresh meat. I was a walking slab of tenderloin when I began teaching, a teacher so raw I was amazed when I opened my first class ever by telling the kids to sit down, and they actually obeyed. When they did, I literally turned my back on them for a moment, realizing with a rising sense of disbelief that this was the first time in my life when anyone actually looked to me as an authority figure, and I was entering a reality I felt wholly unprepared to face. My lack of confidence in my skills as a teacher and my inability to convey a sense of mastery in the classroom undermined any effort to conduct an orderly classroom, and I spent the entire year trying to counteract the negative impression my initial insecurity created. Contrast that with the mind-set of this master teacher, who commanded the classroom with an undeniable air of authority: "You are so confident in what you are doing it is like a high in a sense. I can walk into the classroom, and the kids know from the way you handle yourself that you care and that you can make a difference." What's the line from the song in *The King and I*?—"When I fool the people I fear, I fool myself as well." Even if a novice teacher lacks the confidence to demand his or her students' focus, acting as if she knows what she is doing is the first step toward convincing the kids that they need to toe the line. Too many teachers ask for the students' cooperation and attention instead of expecting it. Whenever I heard a new teacher pleadingly say something like, "I would really appreciate it if you all would pay attention," I knew she was in trouble.

The dirty secret of the classroom is that kids have more power than they know. With their lackadaisical attitude, they can bruise a struggling teacher. With their defiance, they can crush him or her. A veteran teacher made a joke of that reality with his students but recognized that he had little power to gain control if they did in fact ever openly choose to ignore him.

I even kidded with some of the kids I got to know. I would say, "Do you know the power you guys have?" My nightmare is that I would walk into a classroom and say, "Take out your books" and the kids would say, "Nah." I would say, "Take out your books! I told you to take out your books!" They'd say, "Nah." I'd say, "Please, please because I really want to teach. For God's sake take out your books." They'd laugh, but I'd say, "You really

do have a lot of power." With certain teachers that are vulnera-
ble they figure that out, and if they don't like you they go for it.

The principle is simple. Teachers must command the room. Their demeanor can be friendly or intimidating, quiet or forceful, but teachers must convey the unspoken sense that they are in control, and though they may exercise that control lightly, there can be no question who is in charge.

Assign Work That Really Matters

One of the key barometers I used to gauge whether or not my students were engrossed in what we were doing was the frequency with which they asked to go to the bathroom. On days The Conversation was flowing and the ideas were bursting from the students like treats from a birthday piñata, no one wanted to leave the room for a bathroom break. But when I gave a test, I could anticipate that at least a third of those who finished early would develop a sudden, uncontrollable urge to pee, an urge that had little to do with the condition of their bladder but everything to do with their restlessness. Teachers looking to keep classroom interruptions and discipline concerns at a minimum should recognize that a key component in maintaining order is simply to ask questions and create activities that evoke their students' curiosity. That is the point Jim DeLisle makes in his *Education Week* article, "To Jon, on His First Year of Teaching."

> *Kids misbehave in class because what teachers are asking them to do is either too easy, too hard, irrelevant, or boring. I have learned that teachers who know their material and how to present it, who relate the content to students' lives, plan twice as much material as they think they will need for a lesson . . . have few discipline problems. Classroom control is a matter of engagement. If you love what you do and show this to students daily, you are conveying respect for their minds and time—and most of them will engage you back.[1]*

Most kids really do want to learn and thirst for moments of genuine connection. That is why the sheer repetition of facts, formulas, and concepts must at times give way to The Conversation both to facilitate student learning and to stimulate their interest. That is why telling the students why they are learning what they are learning matters so much. That is why busy work—endless worksheets, written assignments that will never be graded, and fifteen math problems when ten would suffice—proves so maddening to the kids. When students wrestle with real concerns they care about, when they get a chance to ask the kinds of questions that give light to an issue they wonder about, students' requests to visit the bathroom are limited to genuine emergencies, and the need to send a misbehaving student to the principal's office diminishes sharply.

So how does a teacher keep a class in hand? Effective classroom management lies on a foundation of a healthy student-teacher relationship, one in which the teacher seeks to understand the stresses an adolescent faces, communicates expectations clearly, and deals with whatever problems arise firmly but without making his or her response seem punitive. As one longtime former administrator who dealt with discipline issues says, "Discipline should be about restoration, not punishment. Teachers who miss that, who think it is about punishment, that's where it becomes a battleground." If teachers want their students to act responsibly, then they need to set the tone for the class and react with wisdom and self-control when the classroom atmosphere goes sour. Reflecting on what she learned about classroom management during her years as a drama and speech teacher, one former educator came to understand her own responsibility to create a climate in which her students would work with her, not against her.

> *I had to develop more resilience, more flexibility. I became slower to react and to draw conclusions about a situation. I didn't inflexibly confront as fast as I did as a new teacher. . . . I still wanted a respectful atmosphere, but my fuse was longer as the years went on. You needed to be. You had to be. It was a better classroom atmosphere. If you wanted your students to be more thoughtful and to think more before they reacted, then you have to model that behavior.*

But the truth is that no one ever entirely gets a handle on classroom management. No matter a teacher's experience, wisdom, or moxie, some kids will have the final say, or at least try to, so a dose of humility is an essential part of a teacher's mind-set. One of the retired teachers was named his district's Teacher of the Year, but even that honor did not safeguard him from the ongoing battle of wits with one of his toughest students.

> *I was really struggling with trying to reach him. I tried being firm to being his best friend. The day before I found out I was Teacher of the Year he came in with about a minute left before lunch—we had a split period—and the bell rings. The kids are all leaving for lunch, and he is starting to walk out and I said, "Whoa, where are you going?" He said, "It is lunchtime." I said, "No, I am going to have you do what the other folks were doing in here for the last twenty-five minutes." I got him to start working. I locked the room up because the girls left their purses, and the other kids left all their book bags. I left for about a minute and a half to get a bag of Cheerios, and in the minute and a half he had gone through all the girls' purses and had gotten about four sets of car keys. After class he went straight out to the parking lot and stole a Grand Cherokee for the weekend. So at the high point of my teaching when people are looking at me as the glory of [our district] I had probably the worst experience of my career.*

Students like this delight in pushing the limits, and no teacher will ever escape those moments of utter frustration when a student or a class gets out of hand. But the truth is, the principles of effective classroom management are actually not much different from the principles that define good parenting. On those random occasions when young moms or dads ask my wife or me for parenting advice, our standard response is really quite simple: make sure your kids know that you love them no matter what, and when you say no, mean it. That's the foundation for good parenting. Those two ideas are an essential part of the foundation for good teaching too. Earning the students' respect is the first and most important step in winning over a class, and the rest flows from that. When kids know a teacher is on their side, the battle is half won. Every student who walks into a classroom asks the same question as Norman Rockwell's little girl: Do I measure up? Teachers who can help their students believe they really do not only minimize the potential for classroom conflict but have given their students an incalculable gift as well. The battles are never going to go away, but teachers who define their limits, let kids know they mean business, and show them they care will reduce most of those battles to minor skirmishes.

Reflections

1. How well do you know your students? What can you do to better understand what matters to them?
2. How do you communicate that you are on the side of the students? What does that mean to you?
3. What policies and procedures do you need to define and articulate to ensure that your class will run smoothly?
4. How often does emotion enter into your confrontations with students? What steps can you take to make sure that the feelings do not escalate?
5. Do students feel that the work you give them to do is busy work? Are they correct in that assessment? What can you do to eliminate that belief?

Action Items

1. Which teachers in your school seem to control their classes and connect with kids seamlessly? Sit down with them and pick their brains about their philosophies and approaches to determine how their approach might inform your own.
2. Look at the list of questions on page 136–37. Go through that list and establish a procedure for each of those concerns that you feel need attention in your own classroom.

Chapter Eight
Teaching with Passion

After spending forty-one years in the classroom, my mind is a muddle of long-forgotten lessons, half-remembered student names, and anecdotes that improve with each retelling. But some long-ago moments at school proved so visually striking that nothing can erase the vivid image they have etched into my brain; some stories are so out of the ordinary that there is no reason to jazz them up when telling them over and over again. A case in point: Walking down the hallway during my planning period many, many years ago, I saw a group of three or four students huddled outside a teacher's doorway staring through the door's window in bemused wonder at the scene unfolding on the other side of the glass. Curious, I stopped to see what had drawn their attention and witnessed a scenario that seemed like it must have been staged. The teacher stood leaning on his desk in front of twenty-plus students, lecturing nonstop in a robotic monotone about some evidently uninteresting point while the two students nearest to him sat in rapt attention, eagerly scribbling down every word he uttered. To a person, the rest of the students lay comatose, sprawled in every imaginable contortion with their heads drooling on their desks and their bodies limp with slumber. I insisted this had to be a joke, that the teacher and his students were conspiring in a prank designed to draw a crowd, but the kids in the hallway adamantly maintained that this was in fact nothing more than an extreme example of what was the norm in this man's class—students viewed it as an opportunity to catch up on their sleep, and the teacher seemed more than willing to let them nap uninterrupted. The sight of a roomful of sleeping kids was stunning, and the message was deeply disturbing. This man had little interest in teaching and even less in his students' welfare.

The truth is that school can be boring enough even without educators who have totally surrendered their responsibility to the kids in their classes. At their worst, bad teachers torture their students, who must endure a bland barrage of information they deem useless, as this senior *Calvin and Hobbes* essay attests.

> *My worst class was [just like] the class in* **Ferris Bueller**[**'s Day Off**]. *In that class we were constantly drilled with information and then had to give that same information back to the teacher without reflection or analysis. The teacher just sat and talked to us about things that were completely irrelevant to us every day, all day, for fifty-five minutes. Our homework every night was to read a chapter in the book and then take a quiz on it the next day. I think I can safely say that I do not remember one thing about that class except my two best friends and I doodled and played tic-tac-toe. Every day I asked myself, "Why am I learning this stuff?" or "Will I ever need to know this?" It never mentally challenged me; it only put me to sleep.*

Though I remember little of my undergraduate education classes, I do recall one statement a professor made in challenging us to bring passion and creativity to the classroom: "It's a sin to bore a kid." If education is indeed about invoking curiosity, if it is about encouraging a sense of wonder and inciting the imagination, then she was surely right. Teachers who resort to endless worksheets and uninspiring lectures as their modus operandi poison the power of learning. I used to sit in my junior-level biology class in high school silently screaming at the teacher in utter frustration as he droned on endlessly and mindlessly about concepts he himself seemed to care little about. I remember thinking at the time, "If he doesn't care, why should I?" That is a question no student should ever have to ask.

Teaching as Salesmanship

The importance of bringing life to the classroom through an animated injection of passion cannot be overstated. While my biology teacher crushed my interest in science, my geology teacher my freshman year of college revived it through his energy and obvious love for his subject. Though I cared nothing for rocks and knew even less about them, this teacher's enthusiasm made each class a dynamic exploration of the earth's formation that captivated me despite my innate disdain for science and my initial resistance to his zeal. The man loved teaching, the man loved the mysteries of earth, and he loved opening our eyes to the beauty all around us, a beauty I had spent the first eighteen years of my life walking blindly by, oblivious to the secrets each rock contained. I loved his class—even though I am as far from being a scientist as a man could possibly be—simply because this teacher's intensity captured me. More than forty-five years later I can still provide at least an amateurish recall of the rocks around me because of this man's gift. His approach to the classroom embodied the spirit identified by Robert Fried in *The Passionate Teacher* as one of the keys to successful instruction: "When I ask myself what makes the greatest difference in the quality of student learning—it is a teacher's passion that leaps out. More than knowledge of subject matter. More than variety of teaching techniques. More than being well-organized or friendly or funny or fair."[1]

The best teachers understand that their job is to sell their subject, that an implicit goal for their classroom is to instill in their students a sense of why this skill, this idea, this controversy really matters and so create a hunger to engage with it. As Michael Sandel, a Harvard political theorist says, teaching is "above all about commanding attention and holding it. Our task is not unlike that of a commercial for a soft drink or any other product. For the most part we want to hold the attention of students for the sake of changing the things they are likely to pay attention to most of the time."[2] To do that, teachers must communicate their love for the subject both in the materials they present and in the manner in which they present them. In "Inspiring Teachers to Excel," Brenda Manning makes the case that part of a student's success in the classroom is generated by the teacher's persona: "Monotone half-dead teachers do not engender inspired students. Energy begets energy, enthusiasm is contagious, and inspired teachers inspire others to excel."[3]

Make 'Em Laugh

At its most basic level, passion in the classroom begins with a teacher's ability to incorporate a sense of humor into his or her daily approach. The ability to monitor a class's body language and adjust immediately once it is clear their attention is dwindling is one of the essential strategies good teachers ideally develop, and a quick dose of humor is one of a teacher's best weapons to bring wandering minds back onboard. Too many times I sat in a classroom observing a young teacher who had obviously lost the class. Students nodded off, doodled incessantly, or surreptitiously texted underneath their desks, yet the teacher plowed on helplessly, fecklessly, simply because he or she did not know how to re-energize the room. The most immediate antidote to that dilemma is humor; kids are so hungry for anything that alleviates the drudgery of school that they regard those teachers with even an ounce of genuine wit as a comic genius worthy of a ten-minute spot on Jimmy Fallon. As one of the retired teachers says, "You have to have a sense of humor. Being serious all the time is just depressing. You have to have fun, you have to create an environment where the kids want to be there. Even if they don't want to learn the material they think it is ok to be in there if you can make it fun for them." Some teachers are expert storytellers, like a poor man's Chris Rock. Some find comedy in the day-to-day routine of life, like a minor league Jerry Seinfeld. Some find humor in the absurd, like a Tina Fey wannabe. Some are masters of the improvisational riff, like a Robin Williams–lite. But even those with no particular comedic gifts can take constant stock of the students' demeanor and act swiftly to shift the mood of the class when lethargy sets in. Here are examples of strategies I have seen teachers adopt when they recognized their students were fading.

- One teacher liked to spontaneously ask his students, "Who would like a standing ovation?" and sent the volunteer out in the hallway. When he or she walked in, the class would erupt in raucous applause, whistling and stamping their feet as the recipient paraded around the room.
- Another teacher jumped to his feet when a student gave an insightful answer to the particularly difficult question,

grabbed two volunteers, and lifted the first student onto their shoulders as the three of them carried him or her around the room to the cheers of the other students.

- Standard procedure for one of our teachers was to hand a dollar to the first student he caught yawning in each of his classes at the beginning of the year to send a message to all his students that it was his responsibility to keep them from yawning.
- One math teacher kept an old table at the front of his room and for years had those students who successfully answered the most difficult problems sign and date the table to memorialize their triumph as the class applauded in recognition of that honor.

Those are hardly the kinds of teaching strategies taught in a graduate education program. The first three are barely pedagogically defensible. But teachers who recognize that the school year is long and that kids need a wake-up call on occasion often resort to a host of techniques to energize the room and give the kids a chance to laugh on those days when tedium seems to be inescapable despite the teacher's best efforts. Almost every teacher I know develops uniquely humorous gimmicks, rituals, and traditions as a way to keep the class going when boredom knocks. For instance, for years we celebrated Pie Day on my birthday in February, a day on which I announced that no one should ever graduate from high school without seeing someone get hit in the face with a pie. After recruiting a volunteer, we would traipse outside in the snow, pace off seven steps, and invite someone to take a shot at hitting the volunteer in the face at that distance. Why did I make such an apparent waste of time part of the routine of my classroom? February is a long, gloomy month, one of those stretches in the school year that drags on and on since spring break seems an eternity away. Every time we did it, that slapstick bit of play injected a bolt of energy in the classroom that got us through the week, gave the kids a laugh, and helped to bond the class together with one of those memories that will linger long after the lessons on subordinate clauses have faded. That stunt had a carryover effect as well. The ability to laugh together helps to build a sense of community in the classroom, and students who feel comfortable with one another and feel a bond with their teacher are more likely to engage in The Conversation, the creative back-and-forth of discussion that helps a class come alive. That is the point that Genelle Morain makes in "Humor as a Welcome Guest in the Classroom."

> *I found that teaching a course where humor is welcomed created a climate in which students knew and liked each other, felt free to express diverse opinions, shared anecdotes that added important dimensions, conducted research they really cared about, asked each other questions, taught me things I didn't know, and laughed whenever they felt like it.[4]*

The types of gimmicks outlined above are acts of semi-desperation, tricks to be utilized only when, despite a teacher's best efforts, he or she simply cannot evoke a response from her students. Bad weather, the big game, the approach of the prom, or the fatigue that sets in during a week in which students face test after test can drain the kids of energy and make even the most creative teacher struggle to connect. Those are the moments when teachers go for the cheap laugh, the old reliable stunts they turn to as a last resort.

Great Expectations

But the passion that matters, the passion that truly makes a difference is based upon far different criteria, as Lief Carter makes clear: "The classroom must engage and stimulate. It must be fun. Not fun in the gimmicky way that panders in order to win popularity contests, but fun in the sense of being unforgettably challenging."[5] It is not enough to be funny. It is not enough for a teacher to know the curriculum well. It is not even enough to write carefully crafted lesson plans with clear learning objectives and assessments that support those objectives. In addition, teachers must accept the responsibility of generating meaningful, demanding work for their students, of helping them to understand the power of ideas through creative pedagogical strategies and personal enthusiasm. The onus is on the teacher to establish a stimulating environment that engages kids and to refuse to settle for a lackluster atmosphere that makes learning a chore. That is the challenge Todd Whitaker issues in *What Great Teachers Do Differently*.

> *Great teachers have high expectations for students but even higher expectations for themselves. Even the worst teachers have high expectations for students. They expect students to be engaged no matter how irrelevant the material, expect students to pay attention no matter how boring and repetitious their classes, expect students to be well behaved no matter how the teacher treats them. The variable is not what teachers expect of the students; the variable is what teachers expect of themselves.*[6]

For some teachers that means being a human perpetual motion machine who commands the room with a level of energy worthy of an otter at play. One of the former teachers ended each week exhausted after spending six periods a day prodding his kids to keep going.

> *I never sat down. It was very important to me that every kid connected with me, so I would never have a kid put his head down because I would do things to get their attention. . . . It might be, "Hey, how are you doing? Are you with me? You've got to help me out!" All those pieces of energy were part of it. When I was finished with the day I was sucking air. I would never sit down, even when they were doing tests, I would be moving, I would be watching, helping out, cajoling, doing whatever.*

Others find sheer joy from being in the classroom and radiate a sense of their excitement through their interplay with their students. These three teachers all emphasize the contagious pleasure they got from being with teenagers each day.

> *I loved coming in the door every morning, and my kids knew it. I loved it. I got to come every day and play with the kids in my classroom. I can't think of anything else I would rather do.*

> *Passion is the essence of teaching. I think you absolutely have to love what you are doing before you can convey it to someone*

*else. The passion I have for **Romeo and Juliet**—the language and the ideas . . . it did not take them a split second to buy into that. I always cry, but I think that was good for them because I wanted them to see that these things touch me, and I wanted to convey that. This is important to me. It is important that I share this with you. It's important to your life. If you can't recite Shakespeare, ok, but your life has been touched by it in some way. I don't think you can be a good teacher without being passionate. Going into a classroom and being rote—just having the attitude that we are going to get through this. Where is the beauty in that?*

I have a passion for teaching. I woke up every morning, and I couldn't wait to go to school. I think it is just who I am. I didn't have to get up and talk myself into it. When I was interviewing for administrative jobs, I was asked, "How do you make yourself get up?" I said I didn't have to make myself get up. I just wake up, and my head is spinning with ideas and schedules. I am anxious to get there.

Another teacher was energized by the opportunity to expose his students to ideas and information that would give them a more vibrant picture of the world. Recognizing that his students' experience was limited, he longed to open their eyes to the questions he hoped they would spend the rest of their lives unraveling: "I am going to bring passion to what I do, passion for the world. What a great world we live in! There is so much interesting stuff. I wanted my kids to be passionate enjoyers of life with a highly developed sense of curiosity." That desire to focus on questions, not answers, is another element Robert Fried identifies in "The Heart of the Matter" as essential in awakening students' sense of wonder and in helping teachers remember why their influence matters so much.

Students need us, not because we have all the answers but because we can help them discover the right questions. It's not that we always know what's good for them but that we want to protect them from having to face life's dilemmas in ignorance or in despair. Those adults to whom young people look for advice on serious life issues know how important they are to kids' futures. For all teachers, the recovery of passion can mean a recovery of our dynamic and positive influence in the lives of children.[7]

That positive influence can take many forms. One of the teachers I interviewed suffered a debilitating stroke at the age of thirty-nine that robbed her of the ability to write and speak. Driven by her desire to serve as an inspiration for those students in her class dealing with their own disabilities, she pushed herself to regain those capabilities through hours and hours of grueling therapy so that she could return to the classroom and provide a positive role model for them. The idealism that drives a woman like this stems from a passionate commitment to lift the hearts and the minds of her students both in what she teaches and in what she represents. Teachers who believe in their students and who communicate that message through the rigor of their curriculum and the intensity of their dedication to their students' success refuse to let the kids in their class fall by the wayside, as this former teacher suggests.

> *When I had a kid say, "I can't do it," I always worried. I am still worried. Can I get through to this kid? There was always that intrigue. The power we retain is on a thread. That's the thing that is so amazing. When our kids have that apathy today, you have to believe for them, and that's what I am afraid some of our younger teachers don't have—the idealism and that realization that you have to believe for them.*

Real Success Is Their Success

For many teachers, that belief translates into the recognition that their success is measured not by any honors they receive or promotions they might earn but by the growth evidenced in the lives of their students. In fact, one of the retired teachers, a man who won a prestigious regional teaching award for excellence, said as much: "When I won that award, I was embarrassed. It was nice to be noticed, but I couldn't help thinking of all the kids I had failed to reach." A highly successful former speech and debate teacher, a man whose students regularly flourished in both state and national competitions, found his satisfaction not in the championships his best students won but in the day-to-day progress he was privileged to witness.

> *I felt lucky that so many kids could demonstrate that visible improvement or auditory improvement in their communication abilities, so that is what kept me going. It was not trophies or that kind of stuff. . . . You were happy for the kids who were state champions and national qualifiers, but to me the most gratifying thing were the kids who grew. One kid lost his first twelve debates in a row, but then he won his thirteenth debate. He became one of the best debaters I had. It wasn't that he brought home all the trophies but he grew in his confidence, in his ability to communicate with people.*

His wife, a much-honored former English, speech, and drama teacher at a neighboring high school, echoes the same sentiment as she describes what motivated her to keep going for so many years.

> *The students who never thought they would be able to explain what they were trying to defend, but they did and they just looked so proud of themselves. Or the student who loved to sing and wanted to be a recording artist. When she was singing she had stage presence out the wazoo, but when you asked her to give a speech she was petrified, but when you let her sing a speech, she realized she could do it. Those were little victories, but those were the ones you remember. Maybe it was somebody who finally understood how to write a five-paragraph essay or learned to portray a character who was just so angry on stage. . . . It is the little victories you remember the most. That's when you knew you had made a difference. It didn't always happen, but it made you keep going for the next time it did.*

Both of these teachers point to the critical truth about the role of passion in education. The real challenge for teachers—and their ultimate objective—should be to help students unearth *their own* passion.

If school is designed to enable young people to discover their talents, to discover their gifts, and to discover whatever it is that makes them come alive, then the passion that matters is that which stirs a student's soul, that evokes an epiphany within that enables a student to, as Ken Robinson writes in *The Element*, "find early in life the work that for you is play."[8] Though those moments come only rarely, the best times in a teacher's life are those in which a student stumbles upon their gift, when they suddenly find delight in an ability they not even know they had. This is how Willa Cather describes those moments of insight in *My Antonia*: "That is happiness; to be dissolved into something complete and great. When it comes to one, it comes as naturally as sleep."[9] The truly life-changing teachers are those men and women who invest so totally in their students that they enable at least a few of them to indeed find their "happiness." They are the kind of educators Robert Fried describes in *The Passionate Teacher*: "Of some of our teachers we remember their foibles, their mannerisms, of others their kindness and encouragement, or their fierce devotion to standards of work we probably didn't share at the time. But of those we remember most, we remember what they cared about and that they cared about us and the person we might become."[10]

One of the great teachers I have known exhibited that kind of investment and witnessed that kind of awakening as she worked with a group of students preparing for the FIRST Robotics Competition the first year our school entered that contest. A young man who was notoriously unfocused and undisciplined in his approach to academics joined the team and spent hour after hour perfecting the robot with his friends under the guidance of this teacher. Captured by the challenge of creating a working machine from scratch, he became wholly absorbed in the task, so much so that he spent long nights at school and Saturday afternoons as well. This indifferent learner, this previously average student, was so excited by robotics that he totally reconfigured his plans for the future, ultimately choosing to major in engineering in college and excelling there despite his so-so high school transcript. This teacher provided the catalyst for this student's life-changing awakening by dedicating her nights and weekends to the robotics team for weeks at a time. Her passion *for* him stirred a passion *within* him.

Another teacher at our school has so captivated his students with the intrigue of constitutional government that literally dozens of them have reframed their college majors, choosing to focus on political science and finding jobs working in the national headquarters of both of the major political parties, in network news divisions, and even in the White House. This man's intensity is contagious and has ignited that same kind of passion in more students than he can ever know. To witness a student's awakening is a gift, one that happens only when teachers themselves are truly excited about what they teach. Robert Gardner, in *On Trying to Teach*, identifies the critical element these teachers bring to the classroom.

> *Appoint any energetic man or woman to the teacher's job and in short order that teacher will regard as indispensable whatever he or she chooses to teach and whatever method by which he or she chooses to teach it. The true teacher will always find something that needs to be taught, the method by which it needs to be taught, and the person who needs to be taught what that teacher regards necessary to teach by that necessary method. The true teacher never rests.[11]*

These are the teachers who change lives. These are the men and women who enable students to perceive a sense of their future and offer them the tools to achieve that dream. They are the ones who light brushfires of hope in students' hearts that affect those students to the end of their days. Here is how Fried describes these teachers in "The Heart of the Matter."

> *Passionate people are the ones who make a difference in our lives. By the intensity of their beliefs and actions, they connect us with a sense of value that is within—and beyond—ourselves. Sometimes that passion burns with a quiet, refined intensity. Sometimes it bellows forth with thunder and eloquence. But in whatever style a teacher's passion emerges, students know they are in the presence of someone whose devotion to learning is exceptional. It's what makes a teacher unforgettable—this caring about ideas and values, this fascination with the potential for growth within people, this fervor about doing things well and striving for excellence.[12]*

The impact of that kind of commitment is incalculable. While caught up in the day-to-day routine of the classroom, it is difficult for most teachers to recognize the impact they are having, but as one of the retired teachers suggests, with the passage of time comes perspective on the difference a life of passionate investment can make.

> *I realize that was my mission in life—to work with young people and make a difference in their lives. It was rewarding. It was very, very rewarding to see a young person who was struggling in accounting or with a computer or in basketball or in life in general to know you are making a difference for him and the world. I never got that philosophical about it at the time, but looking back forty-four years later, I think, "Wow, that was really neat!"*

Taking Care of Business Means Taking Care of Yourself

There is, however, a downside to passion. Some teachers care so much about what they do on behalf of their students that their whole identity is defined by what goes on in the classroom and so allow their sense of self to be determined by a group of fifteen- or sixteen-year-olds. Teaching matters, to be sure, and good teachers devote untold hours of time and levels of emotional energy to making a difference, but setting limits on one's investment in the classroom is a necessary component in maintaining any healthy sense of emotional balance and perspective. One of the retired educators, a man who taught for more than twenty years before becoming a principal, admits he never found that balance and tried to give the teachers in his building permission to limit the time they spent thinking about school.

> *I took the whole thing way too seriously from the very beginning to the very end and didn't have the balance in my life I should have had. That's the way it was when it started and that's the way it was till the very end. I was still getting to school at seven and staying till nine o'clock. It was crazy. What do I wish I had*

learned? I never learned it. I should have been more balanced. And I would talk to teachers about it, giving them permission to find balance. This is just a job, not their life. There were a lot of teachers who were fanatics. They're the kind of teachers you want, but you have to give them permission. They don't really have to get the essays back the next day.

Finding the sweet spot between passion and balance can be a struggle for those who care most deeply about making a difference. Bringing the appropriate degree of commitment into a classroom that changes kids' lives takes a toll, so teachers need to give themselves permission to walk away when weariness threatens to drag them down. The first year I taught I spent so many late nights slaving over what I would teach the next day that I had no time for friends, family, or even sleep. I can't name one television show that aired during 1973, and Watergate was barely a blip in my consciousness. My life was so out of whack that it is a miracle I ever returned to the classroom for year two. But if teachers can establish parameters that allow them to give themselves to the task of teaching but can still step back when they must, then they can perhaps be the kind of educators whose passion infuses the lives of teenagers for decades. And they might be the kind of educators who can reflect on their careers with the same kind of satisfaction expressed by this retired history teacher.

It is a life well spent. That sounds platitudinous, but you think about our short time here and what have you really done. There are a lot of days you make 5 percent of your students miserable, and 85 percent are fine and 10 or 15 percent you touch, and I feel pretty good about that. I enhanced people's lives. It chokes me up to say that. It gives me a good feeling to know that we have made the world a better place with integrity and kindness and rigor.

That's the power of passion. That's the legacy of a man who committed his life to walking into the room each day determined to provoke, cajole, inspire, and enlighten his students. This is a man who can look back on his life and know he made a difference. That's the mark of a great teacher.

Reflection

1. What teacher behaviors did you experience in middle or high school that communicated the teacher's lack of interest?
2. Conversely, what behaviors did you experience in middle or high school that communicated the teacher's passion for the subject, for students, and for teaching in general?
3. Why are you a teacher? Will that motivation/those motivations be enough to keep you hungry to improve for the next five years? Ten years?
4. What are the warning signs that you are devoting too much time to teaching and not enough to your other priorities?

Action Items

1. What questions will your students have about tomorrow's lesson? List those questions that you think will arise from the day's lesson. How can you use those questions to stimulate their curiosity and want them to know more?
2. Who are those veteran teachers in your building who most clearly love teaching? Talk to them about how they have maintained their zeal for so many years.
3. Talk with your spouse, your significant other, or your best friend and ask him or her to help you gauge the balance or lack of balance you bring to your career.

Chapter Nine
Assessments That Make a Difference

In his children's book *Fish Is Fish*, Leo Lionni writes of the great friendship between a tadpole and a minnow, two animals that share a pond in perfect harmony until the tadpole begins his transition to a frog by growing legs and developing a hunger to experience life on dry land. Upon his departure, the now-grown fish longs for his missing friend and wonders if he will ever see him again. After weeks of separation, the frog returns with a splash and regales his friend with tales of life beyond the pond, telling him of

Illustration from FISH IS FISH by Leo Lionni, copyright © 1970 and renewed 1998 by Leo Lionni. Used by permission of Alfred A. Knopf, an imprint of Random House Children's Books, a division of Penguin Random House LLC. All rights reserved.

the "extraordinary things" he has seen—birds who have "wings and two legs and many, many colors," cows who have "four legs, horns, eat grass and carry pink bags of milk," and people who wear clothes and walk upright. As the frog details these incredible sights, the fish pictures what his friend is describing, imagining, in each case, birds, cows, and people with the body of a fish. Limited by what he knows and what he has seen, he cannot even begin to visualize the reality of life outside the pond and so totally misses the truth of what his friend is explaining.[1]

Lionni's ingenious children's story ought to serve as a warning to educators. Because one of the jobs of a teacher is to make the unfamiliar familiar to students with little or no background in the material being presented, the possibility that what she is communicating will be misunderstood is incredibly high. Unless teachers recognize the importance of confirming that their students are in fact keeping up, the chances are that at least some students will be hopelessly lost simply because what they hear is not what the teacher is saying. Communication in the classroom can be as slipshod as that which occurs in the telephone game children play in grade school. As a whispered message is passed from child to child, the words get increasingly distorted, so much so that the message at the end bears little resemblance to the original words that began the game. I have seen the implications of that reality play out in my own classroom on more than one occasion. Shortly after 9/11, for instance, I developed a unit designed to help the students in my writing class understand the roots of the fundamentalist rage directed against the United States. After researching the topic for several months, I opened the first lesson by talking about the fatwa Osama bin Laden had issued in 1996 declaring war against the West. Minutes into the discussion, one of the girls in the class raised a question I had not anticipated, asking, "Where *is* Islam?" That question opened my eyes to the many assumptions I had made in preparing for the unit. Though in an ideal world a senior in high school would know that Islam is a religion and not a place, and though in the wake of 9/11 the thought that a senior would keep abreast of the unfolding course of that tragedy was not unreasonable, it is also not unreasonable to foresee that the kids would have a lot of questions about an issue our curriculum had largely ignored and that their ignorance might be an indictment of the education we had been providing for them. In assuming that my students had a basic understanding of Islam, I made a mistake that forced me to backtrack quickly and lay a foundation of information I had not thought necessary going into the unit. Had that girl not asked that question, I would have thought she and the others were tracking with me nicely and that I was answering the critical questions the kids had about 9/11. And I would have left a trail of confusion because of those assumptions.

Lessons from the Medical Field

The possibility of such egregious miscommunication highlights a major misunderstanding many teachers have about assessments—a misunderstanding it took me years to correct in my own practice. Too many teachers view an end of unit test or project or essay as the conclusive measure of a student's performance, not as a barometer of what a student has or has not learned to that point, nor as an indicator of the teacher's need to consider his or her response to those results. In the first case, the grade the student receives is sacrosanct, a final measure of his or her progress and an accurate reflection of his or her overall ability. In the second, the grade matters less than the teacher's analysis of it. More than one educational researcher has used the following metaphor to describe the tension between these competing views of an assessment's purpose: some teachers treat a test as an *autopsy*, a postmortem designed to reveal a student's level of achievement so the teacher can put a definitive number in a grade book, while others view it as a *diagnosis* that identifies what he or she does and does not know so that the teacher can address whatever shortcomings or misconceptions the student might have.

In the space of a week a few years ago, I had two separate conversations about test results with teachers at our school that illustrate these two perspectives on assessment. One teacher bemoaned his students' lack of preparation for his class after grading their first test of the year, complaining that they were not prepared for the level of work he expected and wringing his hands in frustration that so many students would do poorly in his class because of their deficiencies. In his view, the students' academic shortcomings were their problem, not his, and he predicted a long, stressful year for them because of their inadequacies in his subject. After giving her students a reading quiz early on in their study of *The Scarlet Letter*, the other teacher discovered that her students struggled to understand the complex sentence structure and grammar of Nathaniel Hawthorne's novel. Her response was not to grumble about her students' weak reading skills but to discern how she could help them read Hawthorne with greater comprehension. Instead of plunging ahead with her original lesson plans, she slowed down, backtracked, and developed a series of strategies to help her students read the novel with insight. The first teacher regarded the results of his initial test as an autopsy; the second regarded her students' results as a diagnosis. One essentially washed his hands of his responsibility to his students; the other fully embraced her duty to help them.

The autopsy approach to assessment betrays a fundamental confusion about the purpose of a test, a confusion that I succumbed to early in my career. The truth is I had not really developed a philosophy of assessment when I began teaching and so had no good answer to the question, "What is a test for?" When I first began, I saw a test as an opportunity to reveal my students' weaknesses, not so that I could help them but because that is how I was tested in high school and believed that was how the game was played. At times I have seen teachers use assessments as a punishment to chastise students for their poor study skills or for daydreaming during class. More commonly teachers use assessments as a motivator to force students to pay attention in the days leading up to a major test. Such confusion about the purpose of assessments is not uncommon, according to Robyn Jackson in *Never Work Harder Than Your Students*.

> *Many of us are still unclear about why we grade, what our grades really mean, and how we can use assessment practices to help our students learn. As a result, we develop assessment practices that can actually interfere with students' learning. When we use grades to control students ("If I don't grade it, they won't do it") or to reward students ("He worked so hard, so I will give him a 'B' for effort") or to punish students ("She turned in her assignment one day late, so she gets a zero"), we undermine our goals and make the grade—rather than learning—the end.[2]*

Regular Checkups

What I finally came to understand is that an end of unit assessment ought to provide students with an opportunity to show off, an opportunity to dazzle with a demonstration of all that they have learned and assimilated over their course of study. But for that to happen, a teacher has to give his students ample occasions to test themselves throughout the unit, ample occasions to measure, consider, and reflect upon what they are learning before the end of unit test. Unless a teacher regularly assesses his students' progress throughout a unit, he has no idea if they are actually learning and may be in for an unhappy shock on the day of reckoning—test day. So a regular routine of formative assessments throughout the life of a unit ought to be one of the standard procedures all teachers embrace. That means that teachers continually seek feedback on their students' progress in ways both formal and informal so that they do not perpetuate the kinds of misperceptions experienced by the fish in the pond. Here is how Richard DuFour, Rebecca DuFour, Robert Eaker, and Thomas Many define formative assessment in *Learning by Doing*.

> *1) The assessment is used to identify students who are experiencing difficulty; 2) Those students are provided additional time and support to acquire the intended skill or concept; 3) The students are given another opportunity to demonstrate that they have learned.*[3]

The traditional way teachers determine if students understand the material being presented is to ask, "Are there any questions?" But the number of students who would prefer to sit in silence rather than have their confusion or ignorance exposed publicly is so astronomically high that the question is often little more than an excuse for the teacher to turn the page. Instead, teachers should check for understanding multiple times throughout each unit—and even each lesson—in an effort to ensure that students actually grasp the information at hand.

The truth is, there is nothing especially mystifying about formative assessment since good teachers have always utilized that strategy. It is not a stretch to suggest that Bronze Age mentors teaching their students how best to mount a wheel gave them multiple opportunities to demonstrate that they had learned that skill in a controlled environment long before turning them loose in a wheelwright's shop and long before anyone ever coined the term "formative assessment." That basic pedagogical practice inherent to sound instruction was old news long before the advent of educational research, so much so that it is hard to conceive of a teacher failing to use this strategy on a regular basis. A choral music teacher will isolate the bass section from the tenors and altos and sopranos and ask that section to sing its part alone to ensure the basses are on key. If he or she hears a problem, he or she will single out individual members of that group and work with them to make sure they know their part. A geometry teacher will explain how to find the area of a rhombus and then circulate throughout the room checking to see that the students can solve the sample problems they have been given. A Spanish teacher will ask students to write a two-person dialogue in which one character asks the other for directions to the train station and then have students come to the front of the room to read their exchanges aloud. Before I had ever heard the term "formative assessment," I made it a regular practice in my literature classes to close the period by asking a few students to identify their takeaway for the day so that I could see what the kids seemed to think was the centerpiece of that period's lesson. If time allowed, I would ask each member of the class to write a two- or three-sentence summary of what they thought that day's key teaching point was and collect their reflections as they exited so that I could see if their perspectives matched my intentions. To some degree, in talking about the value of formative assessment, the words of Marcus Aurelius ring true—"We need more often to be reminded than informed"—since that practice is an intuitive part of most teachers' methodology.

The kinds of classroom routines described above are both time tested and presumably universal. But teachers need to know that a highly formalized, regular sequence of formative assessments applied systematically and deliberately can make a major difference in the practice and outcomes of classroom instruction. In fact, Paul Black and Dylan Wiliam make the following claim in "The Formative Purpose: Assessment Must First Promote Learning": "There is strong and rigorous evidence that improving formative assessments can raise standards of pupils' performance. There have been few initiatives in education with such a strong body of evidence to support a claim to raise standards."[4] That makes sense to anyone who agrees that student learning is the be-all and end-all of the classroom. Unless teachers have their finger on the pulse of their students' progress, it is difficult to have any real idea if they are tracking with a teacher's lesson or not.

Only when teachers have some sense of the pace of their students' development can they adjust the tempo and emphasis of their lessons to guarantee that the kids are on target. As Mike Schmoker writes in *Focus*, "Effective teaching requires that we collect informal or formal assessment evidence to make informed adjustments to our instruction. This ensures that the highest possible proportion of students will master the target curricular aim."[5]

How does a teacher collect that kind of feedback? Circulating throughout the room to observe and answer questions when students have class time to work on new material is a given. So are breaking students into groups and sitting in on each cluster as they discuss the idea or concepts under consideration. Asking students to go to the board to solve a math problem or punctuate a sentence as part of a grammar lesson are obvious approaches. But besides the obvious, any number of more focused techniques can be used to measure students' progress. The list below offers at least a cursory catalogue of suggestions ranging from highly informal to highly formal that secondary teachers have used.

- To give themselves a sense of their students' comprehension, several middle school teachers in our school ask their students to give them a thumbs up if they understand the material the teacher has just explained, a thumbs down if they do not, or a thumb turned sideways if they have a specific question.
- Some teachers begin the period by asking students to respond in writing to a prompt or a problem on the board based upon either the previous day's lesson or the reading assigned as homework for the night before. Once the students have been given time to write, the teacher asks several students to share to determine the level of their understanding.
- Math and science teachers in our school have used individual dry erase white boards to determine if their students can solve basic computation problems. The teacher will write a problem on the board in front, ask the students to solve the problem on their personal white board, and invite them to hold their answers aloft so she can check both their work and their steps used in finding their solutions simultaneously.

- Some teachers use clickers to enable students to signal their agreement or disagreement with an idea the teacher presents. Such devices give the teacher automatic statistical feedback that measures students' attitude toward or understanding of an issue or concept.

- Various apps permit teachers to check their students' grasp of the material. For instance, iPad's Showbie allows teachers not only to see how their students are progressing but to comment on their work as well. The Socrative app lets teachers ask broad-based questions like "What part of today's lesson confused you?" or "What questions would you like me to address tomorrow?" as a forum to give students a safe place to confess their confusion.

- A number of web-based sites also give teachers the opportunity to generate quizzes or homework and check the students' progress immediately. The web program Formative enables a teacher to write questions, and once the students have logged in and gotten to work, he can monitor each student's work instantaneously to offer on-the-spot help as needed. Google Forms offers teachers a format to write simple multiple-choice quizzes and will grade those quizzes automatically, providing teachers with prompt feedback on the effectiveness of their instruction.

- Other teachers give frequent low-stakes quizzes over the course of a unit. By assigning students a single algebra problem to solve or an irregular French verb or two to conjugate at the end of a period of instruction, teachers can determine if the kids understand what has been taught so that the teachers can adjust their lesson plans accordingly the following day. Because the students know these grades both count and add up, they have an incentive to listen and ask questions throughout the hour to make sure they understand what is being presented.

That list is hardly comprehensive, and with the proliferation of online and app-based tools, a teacher's options to monitor student achievement electronically will surely grow with each passing month.

But that list does suggest that teachers have a range of options to consider how they will monitor their students' learning so that neither the teacher nor the students blithely sail through the curriculum as if all is well when the reality is that a fair percentage of the students are falling behind.

Informal measures of students' progress benefit the kids as well. If they are frequently assessed when the pressure is off through a series of low-stakes quizzes, students gain a sense of what concepts, skills, and ideas matter most to the teacher and can weigh their own grasp of that material so that they know better both what they must review before a test and what they already know. In *Make It Stick*, Peter Brown, Henry Roediger, and Mark McDaniel clarify the benefits of frequent low-risk assessments for students.

> *This kind of testing . . . increases studying before class, increases attentiveness during class if students are tested at the end of class, and enables students to better calibrate what they know and where they need to bone up. It's an antidote to mistaking fluency with the text . . . for mastery of the subject. Frequent low-stakes testing helps dial down test anxiety among students by diversifying the consequences over a much larger sample: no single test is a make-or-break event. And this kind of testing enables instructors to identify gaps in students' understanding and adapt their instruction to fill them.[6]*

By checking for understanding throughout a unit, teachers serve their students well on several levels. Not only do they maintain an ongoing barometer of their students' progress and give the kids themselves a sense of their own development, but they also force the students to wrestle repeatedly with the key ideas and skills the teacher expects them to master so that they do not surrender to the temptation of waiting until the last minute to cram for the test. Such cramming serves students poorly since doing so does little more than store information in short-term memory. That information vanishes within days of a test, as one of the retired teachers recalls.

> *One of the things I think we struggle with, and I don't think it is just in math, is that we almost train kids to cram and forget. We*

are going to have a test on Tuesday. Learn everything you can and then that's it. One of the kids coined a great phrase—brain dump. You come into a test, brain dump, and it's gone. You've emptied your files. That's not any good. The next year they go into a class and you ask them, what do you remember? They say, "Nothing. It's all dumped."

Using formative assessments systematically to preclude the possibility of a class-wide brain dump makes sense, especially because they help prepare students for the test that will come at the end of the unit, a point the authors of *Make It Stick* identify in their research: "Students who have been quizzed have a double advantage over those who have not: a more accurate sense of what they know and don't know, and the strengthening of learning that accrues from retrieval practice."[7] So not only do formative assessments provide teachers with a window into their students' comprehension, but they help the students prep for the kinds of end of unit tests that will give them an opportunity to demonstrate their mastery of the subject.

Assessments That Work

Learning how to write an effective test, create a meaningful project, or generate provocative essay questions that will help students to demonstrate that mastery are skills few undergraduate education programs emphasize. When I first began to draft my own assessments, I had no idea how difficult to make the tests or how complex to make the writing assignments since I had no sense of the ability of seventh and eighth graders to meet my expectations. Fresh from college and used to reading prose that was largely grammatically correct and coherent, I was shocked by how poorly my students fared when I began to grade their first papers and had to reconsider my standards on the spot. Had a veteran teacher helped me craft an essay prompt that communicated its expectations more clearly, my students would have been more successful, and I would have not had to readjust my sights so radically. That is one reason it makes sense for teachers who share the same teaching assignment to work together to write assessments. Each teacher can serve as a sounding board for the others to ensure that the tests or essays they design are appropriate for the ability level of their students, especially by helping rookie teachers figure out how to make an assessment challenging yet manageable.

Working together to generate assessments makes sense for another reason as well. Inconsistency in modes of assessment on the part of those who teach the same subject may mean that some students seek to transfer from one teacher to another based upon the level of difficulty of the tests in different sections of the same course. If different teachers of the identical course have different grading standards, students in those courses face a hodgepodge of expectations dependent solely upon the whim of their teacher. That is why departments should decide upon consistent policies for testing and grading, including agreement on test retakes and the proper balance between memorization versus analysis. I saw the absurdity of the freedom given to teachers to craft their own assessments in isolation several years ago when I saw copies of the final exams given by two humanities instructors teaching the same class to students on the same grade level. One of the teachers required his students to write a series of complex essays on his final while the other teacher filled his exam with multiple-choice and true-false questions only. Once the word got out that the latter's test offered students a path to an easy A, the registrar faced a horde of students stampeding to transfer into the class with the easier exam. Unless the members of a department hammer out a series of policies to guarantee they all operate according to the same standards, those inconsistencies will damage the department's credibility and drive the registrar insane.

The standard teachers should apply in creating assessments is to ask what kinds of evaluations will best help students demonstrate their mastery of the subject. My world history teacher, the educator I respected most in high school, wrote tests that were challenging but fair. I learned more about his subject by studying for his tests than from any other teacher I had in either high school or college. His standard format for assessment was this: He would give us six or seven possible essay questions with the promise that three of them would be on the test, followed by a list of twenty or so people or events from the time period we were reviewing with the assurance that ten of them would appear on the test in the form of short answer identification. Because of that, we knew what to study and we knew what issues in the

unit he considered most critical for us to know. Since we had to plan for everything on his list, our preparation was comprehensive, and the onus was on each of us to study as much or as little as we felt necessary. His tests gave us an opportunity to show him all that we had learned because he pulled no surprises or unexpected dodges. His tests were as advertised.

Based upon his example, I learned to give the students a series of handouts for each novel or play we would read as each unit began that included the essay they would write at the conclusion of our study. Thus, they knew precisely where they were going from day one. By giving the kids a clear picture of their culminating assessment, they could read the literature with an eye toward the final goal and listen in class for anything that would help them write an effective essay. A retired English teacher carried that principle one step further by giving his students his tests in advance, thus telling them exactly what he expected of them and allowing them to prepare with a clear sense of what he wanted them to know. Initially his strategy elicited a fair degree of skepticism from his students.

> *One of the reactions I got from students was "You are trying to trick us, aren't you? What's the trick?" "It's no trick. These are the things I want you to know for the test. I am going to show you how this works. . . . Then I am going to ask you these questions. The test is going to be on Tuesday," and they'd go, "Well, what are you going to ask us?" and I'd say, "I am going to ask you this, this, this, and this." And they'd say, "What else?" and I'd say, "I haven't taught you anything else." They'd say, "What's the trick?" "There's no trick. This is what I want you to know". . . . We've convinced them there is always a trick. I don't know why we have done that. I always figured it was nuns. They were always tricking me.*

Teachers like this see a test as an opportunity for students to show off, as a chance to demonstrate what they have learned and reveal how effectively the teacher has communicated the key ideas within a unit. Guided by that same approach to assessments, some teachers even go so far as to allow their students to design their own test questions. Shortly before the end of each semester, one of the math teachers in my last school forms his students into groups to write problems they can submit to appear on the final exam. If their questions are chosen, those students who write them receive extra credit on the test. That methodology is supported by Grant Wiggins, who wrote in "The Futility of Trying to Teach Everything of Importance" that "sometimes all a teacher needs to do is ask students to design the questions and tasks composing the final exam based on their knowledge of the essentials."[8] In "The Kind of School We Need," Elliot Eisner makes much the same point.

> *The kinds of schools we need would be staffed by teachers who are as interested in the questions students ask after a unit of study as they are in the answers students give. . . . What would it mean to students if they were asked to raise questions coming out of a unit of study? What kinds of question would they raise? How incisive and imaginative would these questions be? Would the students who do well in formulating questions be the same ones who do well when asked to converge upon a correct answer?*[9]

Though it seems likely that the kinds of questions students generate would give their teachers a sense of how completely they have integrated the key components of a unit into their thinking, most teachers are not willing to go that far. But however teachers view assessments, it is important that they create tests or essay prompts that give the students clear instructions and establish well-defined expectations. Because in my early years I did not tell students exactly what I wanted them to do in responding to a test question or in writing an essay, I received work that fell far short of the standards I had expected—and it was my own fault. Only when I began to be incredibly specific in outlining what I wanted students to do on a test or in an essay did they begin to deliver. If I wanted students to support their argument in each body paragraph with a minimum of two quotes from the short story they were writing about, I needed to tell them so up front. If I wanted them to cite each quote according to MLA standards, it was on me to make that clear. If I wanted them to support each major argument in their body paragraphs with at least two examples, I learned to let them

know. Since students are not mind readers, they appreciated that kind of clarity. Once the kids knew what I expected, they were usually quick to follow through.

I am not the only teacher who has failed to define his criteria distinctly enough and has then struggled to know how to grade the students' responses. For instance, one of our teachers asked this question on a test covering the 1860s: "What were the major causes of the Civil War?" Suppose Student A identifies what she perceives to be the two most important reasons for the war and writes a lengthy essay detailing those points. Suppose Student B identifies nine causes of the war and lists them in bullet form with a brief explanation of each included. Which answer deserves a better grade? Because the teacher did not communicate his expectations, both students have theoretically answered the question, and giving one student a lower grade than the other seems wholly arbitrary and, in fact, unfair. Had the teacher instead asked this question—"Identify what you believe were the two most important causes of the Civil War and, in an essay of at least 750 words, show how those events or people you choose to write about led to the secession of the Southern states"—students would have known how to frame their answers, and the teacher would have a much better sense of how to grade them.

It is also important that teachers' assessments challenge students to make connections, analyze data, and draw conclusions, not simply echo a series of facts drawn from the textbook or a teacher's talking points. A retired history teacher remembers that his early tests focused merely on names, dates, and places but recalls that his assessments grew in sophistication as he matured as a teacher, saying, "I had a number of my more capable students mention how they appreciated the fact that I focused a great deal on the *so what* aspect of testing." He too preferred to give his students options when he tested them and thought it was important to challenge them to wrestle with questions that went beyond rote memory as his understanding of pedagogy evolved.

I was able to craft better assessments. I think about a guy in our department who would write 170 multiple-choice questions. What is number 168 getting at that number 167 missed? I would give students choices. I knew a lot of stuff, but I didn't know everything. So when my teachers would give me the option of answering three out of four, it gave me a chance to show them what I knew. I did that too.

The authors of *Make It Stick* agree that tests that require students to go deeper assist in the learning process more than tests that simply measure recall of information.

> *Tests that require the learner to supply the answer, like an essay or short-answer test . . . appear to be more effective than simple recognition tests like multiple-choice or true/false tests. . . . While any kind of retrieval practice generally benefits learning, the implication seems to be that where more cognitive effort is required for retrieval, greater retention results.*[10]

The *What*, *So What*, and *Now What* in Assessments

One way to force students to go deeper is to ask them to respond to questions that wrestle with the *so what* and *now what* implications of an issue, terms described in chapter four. While tests, projects, and essays should certainly measure students' understanding of vital information central to the core ideas being tested, assessments that enable students to make connections to life beyond school can help them to see that the world of the classroom connects with the world at large. For instance, in a unit on westward migration and the movement to force Native Americans to assimilate into white culture, one U.S. history teacher asked his students to write about examples of assimilation in today's society, identifying both the benefits and the costs for immigrants, minorities, and members of non-Western religions in being asked to conform to the standards of the majority culture. In an ethics class, the assessments the teachers used centered on case studies in which the students were given a series of moral dilemmas and were asked to describe how they would respond to a friend caught in that situation based upon the ethical principles they had studied in that class. As their culminating assessment for their reading of *Heart of Darkness*, students in AP Literature were asked to write an essay in which they chose a contemporary poem, song, movie, sculpture, or painting and then explored its nihilistic overtones to show how they paralleled the themes of the novel to reveal the prevalence of Joseph Conrad's worldview in modern culture. Students in a middle school math class were given the floor plan of a house and asked to determine both the area of each room and the cost of floor coverings for those rooms based upon a list of carpet and tile prices they were given. Assessments that require students both to retrieve the key information discussed in a unit and apply it to concerns that stretch beyond the walls of the classroom make a lot of sense for teachers who want their instruction to be relevant and thought provoking.

That is the approach Grant Wiggins advocates in his call for the use of "authentic assessment" throughout the curriculum. In "The Case for Authentic Assessment," Wiggins compares the best kinds of tests to the two-stage driving test required for teens seeking to obtain their license. The multiple-choice test the teenagers take as part of that process ensures they understand the basic rules of the road; the driving test itself ensures they know how to navigate the streets without sending the townspeople scrambling for cover. Both forms of testing have their place, but the first test without the second would do very little to make the streets safe for the unwary pedestrian. Wiggins includes the following description of the purpose of authentic assessment in that same article.

> *Authentic assessments present the student with the full array of tasks that mirror the priorities and challenges found in the best instructional activities: conducting research; writing, revising, and discussing papers; providing an engaging oral analysis of a recent political event; collaborating with others on a debate, etc.[11]*

In a drama class, authentic assessment might mean asking students to block and direct a scene from a play they have been studying. In a health class, authentic assessment might mean requiring students to undergo a fitness and nutritional analysis that tracks their lifestyle. In an accounting class, authentic assessment might mean that students analyze a business scenario to check for financial improprieties. In a photography class, authentic assessment might mean that students create a portfolio of their work. In my upper-level writing classes, I tried to give students topics to write about that connected with real-life concerns, so they wrote about 9/11, civil rights, affirmative action, and educational issues, along with some lighter assignments to balance the load. One retired English teacher who taught primarily freshmen used her essay assignments to give her students the opportunity to grapple with serious matters that she felt would help them to be both more empathetic and insightful.

> *I wanted them to master the content of being better communicators. I wanted them to be better thinkers because it is such a pivotal year for them in finding themselves and their own identities and interests and friends and even career paths for some of them. A lot of them were evaluating, am I going to believe what my parents tell me to believe or have always believed? Is it the culture I am coming from in my home? They spend the year questioning it all. It is the natural ninth-grade progression. I wanted to give them skills of evaluating that well, asking questions well. How to ask questions and not to be afraid of the questions. Navigating that, they found themselves changing and asking what is right, what is true? What am I going to believe politically? In all the issues of our culture—religiously, what am I going to believe as I am growing and changing? I just wanted to give them skills to know how to navigate those questions.*

After the Test

The kinds of assessments teachers give matter, but so does their response to those assessments once they have been turned in. Teachers who see a test as an autopsy are ready to move on once they have graded it. But for those who see it as a diagnosis, their work is just beginning. Test results give educators a chance to identify what they neglected to teach well or where their students are confused and allow teachers to reset by reviewing whatever material the students have failed to grasp. Like many English teachers, I typically made a list of the most common points of confusion evidenced in the students' papers before I returned a set of essays to a class and addressed those concerns as we prepared for the next assignment. Many teachers allow their students to retake tests, arguing that if the ultimate goal is to encourage all students to learn, then the initial grade the student earns is of little concern relative to the desire to have him master the material at a later date. Those who would argue that students should have learned on the first go-round, that they should have taken better notes, listened more carefully, and studied more thoroughly have a point, but perhaps they should consider the possibility that a wide range of factors can explain a poor grade.

- Maybe the teacher worded a test question poorly. I certainly am guilty of that mistake. I worded an essay question on a final exam so ambiguously one year that I essentially had to disregard the results of that question since the kids did not know how to begin to formulate an answer.
- Maybe the students did study and thought they knew the information. That happened to me when I was a student. I *really* studied for a history final in college and was disappointed that my grasp of the material was not as great as I had thought.
- Maybe the teacher didn't explain what would be on the test clearly enough. Though my own children didn't receive a lot of sympathy from me when they said it, their claims that a test differed significantly from what the teacher had promised were expressed often enough to convince me that their complaints had at least some credibility.
- Maybe the students were afraid to ask for help. I had teachers in high school and college who were so aloof or intimidating that I would never consider going to them for a private tutorial.
- Maybe the teacher sees a pattern of misunderstanding he or she didn't anticipate when grading the test and realizes the students' errors in that section are his or her responsibility.
- Maybe the basketball game went into triple overtime the night before and the star point guard and head cheerleader didn't get home until eleven o'clock, forcing them to work ten calcu-

lus problems, fill out a worksheet for Spanish, and then study for the test until three in the morning.

- Maybe the student is in the midst of a family crisis and cannot concentrate because of the pain he or she is in.
- Maybe the student has been sick but has been coming to school anyway because he or she is so conscientious he or she won't surrender to an illness.

It was not until well into my career that I began to allow students to retake tests, but because my goal was to give students every chance to learn, it finally dawned on me that refusing to give them a second chance made no sense. I had always required students to rewrite their essays for my class, and if that was okay, what possible rationale could I concoct to suggest that a test grade was somehow sacred but an essay grade was not? The unspeakable truth is that grades don't really measure learning all that well anyway, so why not exhibit a degree of flexibility and allow students another shot at showing their stuff?

If the purpose of an assessment is indeed to offer students a chance to demonstrate what they have learned, then teachers should not cavalierly give a test, grade it, and move on oblivious to the outcome of that test. Teaching is a partnership in which the adults are the senior associates, men and women who understand they have a great responsibility to push, to prod, and to cajole their sometimes unwilling junior partners, and to pick them up when they fall down. But the rewards of seeing those kids who struggle the most succeed are immeasurable, a point one of the retired teachers emphasizes.

I learned so much from the kids. If you listen and watch you can pick it up. I have learned resilience from kids, I have learned how to sacrifice from kids, I have learned all kinds of things from observing and being with them. I love the students. I had kids who never should have made it, but they overcame so much.

Recognizing that many of his students regarded school as nothing but endless toil, that same teacher asked his students to write him a letter telling him about themselves for their first assignment,

promising them they would all get an A if they complied. The results of that assignment proved far-reaching.

> *That's all they had to do—write me a letter. And I would tell them if you do that, you'll get a 50 out of 50. The kids would think, "Man, I am pretty good in this class!" I would have kids who would have Ds and Cs getting As the first grading period. I realized that it was a lot easier to hold on to a B or A than to give a kid an F and say "Ok, now move up." It's a lot harder. . . . My kids would go back to their old teachers and say, "Guess what, I got an A in English." There were kids who ended up with Bs or Cs or even As who never got anything above a C prior to that, and they were producing good stuff because once they got hooked they'd say, "What do I need to do to keep going?" There were kids who just needed that. Then my demands and restrictions would become more typical, but they were able to hold on to that first good grade if they got inspired enough.*

That teacher's approach might not make sense to those educators who prefer to take a hard line. But convincing reluctant students that they can learn is part of the battle, and teachers who check regularly to see if their kids are learning, adjust their lesson plans based upon what those formative assessments reveal, design end of unit assessments that smack of authenticity, and provide opportunities for those who are floundering to try again open the door to help all but the most intransigent kids to learn. Isn't that why we are there in the first place?

Reflection

1. What is the purpose of an assessment?
2. What kinds of formative assessments make sense in your subject area?
3. When should an end of unit assessment in your class be an autopsy? A diagnosis?
4. How specific do you believe you should be in telling students how to study for a test?
5. What part do *so what* and *now what* questions play in your assessments?

6. What kinds of assessments frustrated you when you were in middle or high school?

Action Items

1. Rewrite your next assessment to reflect all three steps of the learning process—the *what*, the *so what*, and the *now what*.
2. In designing your next unit, plan a series of formative assessments to be given at critical points in the unit to measure your students' success.
3. Try an experiment: the next time your class does poorly on a test, give them a retest and gauge both their results on the second test and their attitude toward learning going forward.

Chapter Ten
Conclusion

On January 12, 2007, violinist Joshua Bell, a man who routinely plays before sellout crowds throughout the world and who won the Avery Fisher prize as the best classical musician in America that year, conducted an unusual social experiment at the behest of the *Washington Post*. To test whether commuters would recognize the majesty of Bell's musical craftsmanship outside the venue of a concert hall, the *Post* convinced Bell to choose a spot in the L'Enfant Plaza metro station and perform for the men and women who filed through that location on their way to work in downtown Washington, DC. Clad informally in a T-shirt and baseball cap, Bell played a series of classical pieces for forty-three minutes on that cold January day, filling the halls of the Metro stop with the soaring sounds of his $3.5 million Stradivarius as 1,097 people passed through. In advance of Bell's performance, Leonard Slatkin, director of the National Symphony Orchestra, was asked to predict what would happen. Convinced that Bell's mastery of the violin would not go unnoticed, he guessed that a crowd of seventy-five to one hundred would gather and that the commuters would be quick to recognize the magnificence of what they were hearing.

In fact, almost no one noticed. In the nearly three-quarters of an hour that Bell played for those on their way to work, only seven people stopped to listen to his performance for even a minute. The rest hurried by, deaf to the beauty Bell was creating only yards from where they scurried by, heads down and focused on the meetings and phone calls that awaited them once they reached their office. Though Bell had, only three nights before, played to a capacity crowd in Boston and two

188

weeks later would sell out a concert in Maryland, on this day he was in essence invisible, a man creating a cascade of noise that made almost no impression on those who passed by intent on their day's schedule. In his article recounting Bell's experience in the Metro station that day, *Post* reporter Gene Weingarten asked an obvious question, one that has more than a little relevance for education.

> *If we can't take the time out of our lives to stay a moment and listen to one of the best musicians on Earth play some of the best music ever written; if the surge of modern life so overpowers us that we are deaf and blind to something like that—then what else are we missing?[1]*

One of the reasons we struggle so much in this country to gain any sense that our schools are truly effective is that we have such a hard time agreeing on what an education is for. Schools must certainly enable students to develop skills, they must certainly provide them with critical information, they must certainly prepare them for a career, and they must certainly help them to discover their gifts, but one of the priorities we should also place on schools is that they help students to discover what they are missing, to cultivate a sense of curiosity that ensures they do not walk through life blind and deaf to all that surrounds them.

Good teachers can help most students to read and write, add and subtract, and embrace a wide range of other skills relevant to the many disciplines we offer in school. But great teachers go beyond all of that to point their students to the beauty of ideas, to the complexities of thought, and to the marvelous benefits gained through a life that never stops seeking to notice more and know more. It is too easy for all of us to act just as the commuters did on that January day in L'Enfant Plaza, walking nonchalantly by the majesty surrounding us as if it is not even there. Part of a teacher's job is to direct his students' eyes to what is right in front of them, to the day-to-day mysteries they might otherwise remain oblivious to because they are too wrapped up in the minutiae that so dominate their lives. The Roman philosopher Seneca was criticized for pointing out the obvious in so much of his philosophy, but in his mind, that was exactly what a good philosopher—or a good teacher—should do: "People say, 'What good does it do to point out the obvious?' A great deal of good; for we sometimes know facts without paying attention to them. . . . We lose much that is set before our eyes."[2] It is the teacher's job to see that does not happen, to see that students develop a keen eye to look past the obvious to discover the profound.

We began this discussion of teaching by looking at a number of the metaphors our graduating seniors fashioned to describe their worst classes at our school. But those same students were also asked to create metaphors to describe those classes that captured their imaginations and helped them to see beyond the obvious to questions they had never even considered. The two examples below seem to capture the essence of what a great classroom experience should be all about.

> *An appropriate metaphor for many of my best classes is a tornado that gains momentum as it accumulates debris. Some teachers made material so interesting that the more I learned the more I wanted to learn, the more my momentum increased, and the more I picked up. Often in these classes the teachers encouraged the students to spend time thinking about what they were learning and what it meant to them. In these classes I was not told what opinion I should have about the subject, but I was encouraged to research and think until I had formed my own unique opinion. In these classes the teacher was obviously interested in what they were teaching and constantly sought out current, relevant examples of the material to show the class to make it obvious the material was pertinent to our lives.*

> *I think that at best school is an astronomer showing a child something through a telescope. In certain classes, I have felt like both the teacher and I can feel that the other one is genuinely interested in the subject. In those classes, I have engaged the subject and sought to learn it not because I was forced to but because it legitimately engaged me as a human being and not just as a student. I have thoroughly enjoyed those classes and am proud to have the knowledge that I acquired from them still in my brain. The best classes I have had have this astronomer attitude. There was a continual mood of, "You think that was cool? Check* **this** *out!"*

"You think that was cool? Check *this* out!" Isn't that the offer teachers should make to their students every day? Isn't that the hope great teachers extend as they seek to open their students' eyes to the wonder of ideas and the power of the gifts that students carry within themselves? The truth is that once I figured out how to teach even a little, I could help most students become better writers. The truth is that it wasn't that hard to help most students read a piece of literature with greater sensitivity and insight than before. But if the pages of this book have said anything at all, it is that the task of teaching is more than that; it is about helping our students to become more fully human, to become men and women who certainly are good at their jobs but who care about big dreams and bigger visions, who embrace a commitment to life-long learning and the welfare of the community in which they live. School at its best should be a place of exploration and discovery, a place where kids can make mistakes, ask questions, and develop a curiosity about the world that will never leave them. Perhaps Susan Engel's recipe for the classroom articulated in "Joy: A Subject Schools Lack" says it best.

> *Instead of trying to get children to buckle down, why not focus on getting them to take pleasure in meaningful, productive activity, like making things, working with others, exploring ideas, and solving problems. These focuses are not so different from the things to which they already gravitate and in which they find delight. . . . Decades of research have shown that in order to acquire skills and real knowledge in school, kids need to want to learn. You can force a child to stay in his or her seat, fill out a worksheet, or practice division. But you can't force a person to think carefully, enjoy books, digest complex information, or develop a taste for learning. To make that happen, you have to help the child find pleasure in learning—to see school as a source of joy.*[3]

That concept of education seems daunting, but consider the perspectives of these career educators as they reflect on what mattered to them when they stepped into the classroom.

- I felt like if I could enable my students to be better citizens, better scientists, to make wiser decisions when they vote, or to make wiser decisions on the job, then they will make a difference in the world, so through them I am able to make the world a better place.

- I will do whatever it takes to ensure my students have a meaningful experience every single day and that there aren't any minutes that are wasted. What we are doing here is important because I want these kids to make a difference in the world.
- When the hour ends, you know you sent a message. Maybe it was just one little thing, but you said it in such a way that your heart was there. It wasn't just words. You breathed life into words and gave them meaning, and it carries them and you from day to day and year to year.
- There is no more important job than teaching. I've changed. I used to have us number two behind the clergy. I've now moved us ahead of the clergy. I always had doctors at number three. I really believe that.

"There is no more important job than teaching." I think every great teacher secretly clings to that belief. Teaching the use of the semicolon wasn't enough to keep me in the classroom for forty-one years. Grading tens of thousands of essays, researching transcendentalism, and driving home at 10:30 on a 5-degree night after coaching a losing basketball game were not either. Touching kids' lives, trying to pass on the joy of learning, and shaping their passions were what it was all about, for me and for each of the teachers quoted above. Was it worth it? Let the words of one of the most gifted educators I know provide the answer.

> *Absolutely, in a heartbeat. I believe that I was given a great gift, and I have always had a sense that I am doing exactly what God has placed me on the earth to do, and there is nothing else I would rather do. I am very grateful, privileged really. I have made lots of mistakes along the way, but in terms of a career, it has been a gift.*

Shortly after I began to teach I was moved by an excerpt of a letter written by a Holocaust survivor to educators published in *Teacher and*

Child by Haim Ginott. Though I read these words, and Ginott's reflections that follow, more than forty years ago, they served as a touchstone for why I taught for the rest of my career.

> *I am a survivor of a concentration camp. My eyes saw what no person should witness: gas chambers built by learned engineers. Children poisoned by educated physicians. Infants killed by trained nurses. Women and babies shot by high school and college graduates. So, I am suspicious of education.*
>
> *My request is: Help your children become human. Your efforts must never produce learned monsters, skilled psychopaths, or educated Eichmanns. Reading, writing, and arithmetic are important only if they serve to make our children more human.[4]*

Though these words may seem dramatic—and they are—they continued to linger in my consciousness as I refined my core beliefs about teaching, as I considered what to teach, and as I thought about how to teach in the years that followed. I certainly cared about my students' academic success, and I hoped they would find fulfilling, lucrative careers, but that is not why I spent so many years in the classroom. I labored so long hoping that something we did or said or read would resonate within a student's soul and change him or her forever. And the truth is, I had to acknowledge that in most cases I would never even know if that happened. So much of what goes on within a student's mind is invisible, so teaching is at last an act of faith, a point Robert Gardner makes clear in *On Trying to Teach.*

> *My own teachers, looking forward, thought they were teaching me one thing; and I looking back, have incontrovertible evidence they were over and over teaching another. That being the case, though in my own teaching I am certain I have been teaching in accord with students' hidden questions, and though I have felt and cautiously expressed enthusiasm for the benefits of that enterprise, I must admit I lack hard evidence—or even persuasive soft evidence—that I have been doing what I think I have, or, if I have, that my enthusiasm is warranted. If it's true that my teachers did not know what they were teaching, it's true*

*that I do not know what I have been teaching. That is, I know
what I have been teaching; it's only that I have so little notion
what my students have been learning.*[5]

Teaching, then, requires a heavy dose of humility for it is always a mystery, always a journey into the unknown, and teachers will never really know the impact they are having. We walk out the door on the last day of the school year—or the last day of our career—hoping we have made a difference, hoping that our students have learned and grown and become more fully human because of us, but we will never be able to measure the influence we may have had. Technique matters, pedagogy matters, and curriculum matters as well, but what really occurs in the classroom is beyond a teacher's control. One of the teachers I interviewed for this project loved to share with his students a poem by Howard Nemerov, a poem that captures the hope that every parent has for his or her child's teachers and that encapsulates so well the fear and the aspirations and the dreams that education inspires.

September, the First Day of School[6]

My child and I hold hands on the way to school,
And when I leave him at the first-grade door
He cries a little but is brave; he does
Let go. My selfish tears remind me how
I cried before that door a life ago.
I may have had a hard time letting go.

Each fall the children must endure together
What every child also endures alone:
Learning the alphabet, the integers,
Three dozen bits and pieces of a stuff
So arbitrary, so peremptory,
That worlds invisible and visible

Bow down before it, as in Joseph's dream
The sheaves bowed down and then the stars bowed down
Before the dreaming of a little boy.

That dream got him such hatred of his brothers
As cost the greater part of life to mend,
And yet great kindness came of it in the end.

II

A school is where they grind the grain of thought,
And grind the children who must mind the thought.
It may be those two grindings are but one,
As from the alphabet come Shakespeare's plays,
As from the integers comes Euler's Law,
As from the whole, inseparably, the lives,

The shrunken lives that have not been set free
By law or by poetic phantasy.
But may they be. My child has disappeared
Behind the schoolroom door. And should I live
To see his coming forth, a life away,
I know my hope, but do not know its form

Nor hope to know it. May the fathers he finds
Among his teachers have a care of him
More than his father could. How that will look
I do not know, I do not need to know.
Even our tears belong to ritual.
But may great kindness come of it in the end.

That is the hope I had for my own children, the same hope I carried into the classroom each day as I dared my students to explore
ideas and tackle challenges that would take them to places they did
not even know existed when they walked into the classroom on the
first day of school. That is the hope embodied by the men and women
quoted in this book, teachers who gave their lives and poured their
energies into helping their students discover their own dreams and
abilities on the road to becoming ever more human. That is the hope
of all parents who pray that their sons and daughters will encounter

teachers committed to building in their students not only a set of skills but a sense of compassion and vision as well. It is those ends that give a career in the classroom so much meaning and make the experience so rewarding. As one of the teachers said so well, it is indeed a life well spent.

Reflection

1. Who do you want your students to become? How does your approach to teaching help them to reach that end?
2. What are the "cool" elements in your subject area you want your students to see?
3. What were the most important lessons you learned from your best teacher in middle or high school?

Action Items

1. What metaphor would you like your students to use to describe you as a teacher? How do you have to change to make that metaphor become a reality?
2. What do you want your students to remember about your class five years from now? How do your current lessons reflect that hope?

Endnotes

Introduction

1. Lebowitz, *Fran Lebowitz Reader*, 27.

Chapter One: First Year Follies

1. Berliner, "In Pursuit of the Expert Pedagogue," 6.
2. Metzger, "Maintaining a Life," 347.
3. Fuller, "Teaching Isn't Rocket Science: It's Harder."
4. McCann and Johannessen, "Why Do New Teachers Cry?," 138.
5. Benham Tye and O'Brien, "Why Are Experienced Teachers Leaving the Profession?," 31.
6. Wolterstorff, *Educating for Life*, 118.
7. Mencken, "Travail."

Chapter Two: Defining What Really Matters

1. Metzger, "Maintaining a Life," 349.
2. Freire, *Pedagogy of the Oppressed*, 4.
3. Neill, *Summerhill*, 64.
4. Adler, *Paideia Proposal*, 12.
5. Fiske, *Smart Schools, Smart Kids*, 253.
6. Ballard, "Hoops Whisperer," 43.
7. Van Dyk, *Craft of Christian Teaching, 32.*
8. Gardner, *On Trying to Teach*, 93.
9. Brooks, *Road to Character*, xi.
10. Kaufmann, *Sabbatical Report on Christian Schools, 2002.*

Chapter Three: Defining What to Teach

1. Franklin, "Remarks Concerning the Savages of North America."
2. Wood, *A Time to Learn*, 80.
3. Jackson, *Never Work Harder Than Your Students*, 156, 159.
4. Marzano, "Curriculum Design."

5. Wiggins and McTighe, "Put Understanding First," 36.

6. Segal, "Martian Math."

7. Stephenson, *Extraordinary Teachers*, vii.

8. Metzger, "Maintaining a Life," 347.

9. Ibid.

10. Palmer, *Let Your Life Speak*, 11.

Chapter Four: Defining How to Teach

1. Holley, *Teacher's Technique*, 6.

2. Fine, "Ignorance of U.S. History Shown by College Freshmen."

3. Keliher, "Forget the Fads—The Old Ways Work Best," 18.

4. Keliher, "If It Wasn't Around in the Middle Ages, It's a Fad."

5. Pellicer, "Effective Teaching: Science or Magic?," 2.

6. Darling-Hammond, "Teachers and Teaching," 5.

7. Marzano, *Art and Science of Teaching*, 4.

8. Schmoker, *Focus*, 17.

9. Ibid., 15.

10. Duffy, "Teaching and the Balancing of Round Stones," 779.

11. Thomas, "Education's Seven Deadly Myths," 64.

12. Cuban, *How Teachers Taught*, 16.

13. Glynn, "Psychology of Teaching," 95.

14. Wiggins and McTighe, "Put Understanding First," 37.

15. Marzano, *Art and Science of Teaching*, 38.

16. Brooks, "Schools for Wisdom."

17. Graham, *Teaching Redemptively*, 93.

18. Brown, Roediger, and McDaniel, *Make It Stick*, 2.

19. Ibid., 18.

20. Ibid., 30.

21. Wilson, "In Praise of Holistic Teaching," 228.

22. Wagner, "Secondary School Change," 40.

23. Postman, *Technopoly*, 126.

24. Jhally, quoted in "The Ad and the Ego: Official Study Guide," 6.

25. Wood, *A Time to Learn*, 83.

26. Ibid., 87.

27. Brown, Roediger, and McDaniel, *Make It Stick*, 6.

28. Bain, *What the Best College Teachers Do*, 40.

29. Karnok, "Thoughts on College Teaching," 103.

30. Greitens, *Resilience*, 233.

31. Marzano, *Art and Science of Teaching*, 34.

32. Wiggins and McTighe, "Put Understanding First," 37.

33. Darling-Hammond, "Teachers and Teaching," 6.

Chapter Five: Defining How to Improve

1. Barth, *Learning by Heart*, 23.

2. Carroll, "Next Generation of Learning Teams," 13.

Chapter Six: Why Relationships Matter

1. Holt, *How Children Fail*, 92.
2. Sullo, *Motivated Student*, 14.
3. Coenen, "Teaching 'Outside the Box,'" 158.
4. Stephenson, "My Teaching Philosophy and the Teachers Who Shaped It," 257.
5. Ibid.
6. Bain, *What the Best College Teachers Do*, 136.
7. Ibid., 141.
8. Blau, "Magical Teacher."
9. Dawe, "Teaching: A Performing Art," 550.

10. Hendricks, *Teaching to Change Lives*, 84.

Chapter Seven: Understanding Classroom Management

1. DeLisle, "To Jon, on His First Year of Teaching," 34.

Chapter Eight: Teaching with Passion

1. Fried, *Passionate Teacher*, 5.
2. Bain, "What Makes Good Teachers Great?"
3. Manning, "Inspiring Students to Excel," 138.
4. Morain, "Humor as a Welcome Guest in the Classroom," 121.
5. Carter, "Teaching Tricks," 108.
6. Whitaker, *What Great Teachers Do Differently*, 56.
7. Fried, "The Heart of the Matter," 50.
8. Robinson, *The Element*, 7.
9. Cather, *My Antonia*, 27.
10. Fried, *Passionate Teacher*, 13.
11. Gardner, *On Trying to Teach*, 93.
12. Fried, "The Heart of the Matter," 50.

Chapter Nine: Assessments That Make a Difference

1. Lionni, *Fish Is Fish*.
2. Jackson, *Never Work Harder Than Your Students*, 127.
3. DuFour et al., *Learning by Doing*, 56.
4. Black and Wiliam, "The Formative Purpose."
5. Schmoker, *Focus*, 60.

6. Brown, Roediger, and McDaniel, *Make It Stick*, 43.

7. Ibid., 42.

8. Wiggins, "The Futility of Trying to Teach Everything of Importance," 45.

9. Eisner, "The Kind of School We Need," 579.

10. Brown, Roediger, and McDaniel, *Make It Stick*, 41.

11. Wiggins, "The Case for Authentic Assessment."

Chapter Ten: Conclusion

1. Weingarten, "Pearls Before Breakfast."

2. McKay and McKay, "Seneca on the Value of 'Obvious' Advice."

3. Engel, "Joy: A Subject Schools Lack."

4. Ginott, *Teacher and Child*, 91.

5. Gardner, *On Trying to Teach*, 158.

6. Nemerov, *Collected Poems*, 426.

Works Cited

"The Ad and the Ego: Official Study Guide." Online at https://brainmass. com/file/341521/ (accessed November 14, 2003).

Adler, Mortimer. *The Paideia Proposal*. New York: Touchstone, 1998.

Bain, Ken. "What Makes Good Teachers Great?" *Chronicle of Higher Education* 50, no. 31 (April 9, 2004): B7–B9. http://www.chronicle.com/ article/What-Makes-Great-Teachers/31277 (accessed April 9, 2004).

Bain, Ken. *What the Best College Teachers Do*. Cambridge, MA: Harvard University Press, 2004.

Ballard, Chris. "The Hoops Whisperer." *Sports Illustrated*, October 21, 2009.

Barth, Roland. *Learning by Heart*. San Francisco: Jossey-Bass, 2004.

Benham Tye, Barbara, and Lisa O'Brien. "Why Are Experienced Teachers Leaving the Profession?" *Phi Delta Kappan* 84, no. 1 (September 2002): 24–32.

Berliner, David. "In Pursuit of the Expert Pedagogue." *Educational Research* 15, no. 7 (Aug.–Sept. 1986): 5–13.

Black, Paul, and Dylan Wiliam. "The Formative Purpose: Assessment Must First Promote Learning." *Yearbook of the National Society for the Study of Education* 103, no. 2 (June 2004): 20–50; posted on Wiley Online Library on April 4, 2005: http://onlinelibrary.wiley.com/doi/10.1111/ j.1744-7984.2004.tb00047.x/abstract (accessed May 9, 2012).

Blau, Cheryl. "The Magical Teacher." PhD diss., Union Institute, 1993.

Brooks, David. "Schools for Wisdom." *New York Times*, October 16, 2015. http://www.nytimes.com/2015/10/16/opinion/schools-for-wisdom. html (accessed November 2, 2015).

Brooks, David. *The Road to Character*. New York: Random House, 2015.

Brown, Peter, Henry Roediger, and Mark McDaniel. *Make It Stick: The Science of Successful Learning*. Cambridge, MA: Belknap Press, 2014.

Carlson, Ronald L. "Teacher Burnout." In Stephenson, *Extraordinary Teachers*, 125–32.

Carroll, Tom. "The Next Generation of Learning Teams." *Phi Delta Kappan* 91, no. 2 (October 2009): 8–13.

Carter, Lief A. "Teaching Tricks." In Stephenson, *Extraordinary Teachers*, 107–14.

Cather, Willa. *My Antonia*. New York: Penguin Books, 2012.

Coenen, Dan T. "Teaching 'Outside the Box.'" In Stephenson, *Extraordinary Teachers*, 155–60.

Cuban, Larry. *How Teachers Taught: Constancy and Change in American Classrooms, 1890–1990*. New York: Teacher's College Press, 1993.

Darling-Hammond, Linda. "Teachers and Teaching: Testing Policy Hypotheses from a National Commission Report." *Educational Researcher* 27, no. 1 (January 1998): 5–15.

Dawe, H. A. "Teaching: A Performing Art." *Phi Delta Kappan* 65, no. 8 (June 1984): 548–52.

DeLisle, Jim. "To Jon, on His First Year of Teaching." *Education Week* 23, no. 21 (February 4, 2004): 31, 33.

Duffy, Gerald. "Teaching and the Balancing of Round Stones." *Phi Delta Kappan* 79, no. 10 (June 1998): 777–80.

DuFour, Richard, Rebecca Dufour, Robert Eaker, and Thomas Many. *Learning by Doing: A Handbook for Professional Learning Communities at Work*. 2nd ed. Bloomington, IN: Solution Tree, 2010.

Eisner, Elliot. "The Kind of School We Need." *Phi Delta Kappan* 83, no. 8 (April 2002): 576–94.

Engel, Susan. "Joy: A Subject Schools Lack." *The Atlantic*, January 26, 2015. http://www.theatlantic.com/education/archive/2015/01/joy-the-subject-schools-lack/384800/ (accessed October 20, 2015).

Fine, Benjamin. "Ignorance of U.S. History Shown by College Freshmen." *New York Times*, April 4, 1943. http://query.nytimes.com/gst/abstract.html?res=9B0DE4DC1F39E33BBC4C53DFB2668388659EDE&legacy=true (accessed January 12, 2006).

Fiske, Edward. *Smart Schools, Smart Kids: Why Do Some Schools Work?* New York: Touchstone, 1992.

Franklin, Benjamin. "Remarks Concerning the Savages of North America." 1784. http://franklinpapers.org/franklin/framedVolumes.jsp?vol=5&page=121a (accessed January 21, 2007).

Freire, Paolo. *Pedagogy of the Oppressed*. New York: Bloomsbury Academic, 2000.

Fried, Robert. "The Heart of the Matter." *Education Week Teacher*, October 1, 1995.

Fried, Robert. *The Passionate Teacher*. Boston: Beacon Press, 1995.

Fuller, Ryan. "Teaching Isn't Rocket Science: It's Harder." *Slate*, December 18, 2013. http://www.slate.com/articles/life/education/2013/12/teaching_in_america_s_highest_need_communities_isn_t_rocket_science_it_s.html (accessed December 23, 2013).

Gardner, Robert. *On Trying to Teach*. Hillsdale, NJ: Analytic Press, 1994.

Ginott, Haim. *Teacher and Child*. New York: Macmillan, 1972.

Glynn. Shawn. "The Psychology of Teaching." In Stephenson, *Extraordinary Teachers*, 95–100.

Graham, Donovan. *Teaching Redemptively: Bringing Grace and Truth into Your Classroom*. Colorado Springs, CO: Purposeful Design Publications, 2003.

Greitens, Eric. *Resilience: Hard-Won Wisdom for Living a Better Life*. New York: Houghton Mifflin, 2015.

Hendricks, Howard. *Teaching to Change Lives: Seven Laws of the Teacher*. Colorado Springs, CO: Multnomah Publishing Group, 1987.

Holley, Charles E. *The Teacher's Technique*. New York: The Century Co., 1924.

Holt, John. *How Children Fail*. Boston: DaCapo Press, 1995.

Jackson, Robyn. *Never Work Harder Than Your Students*. Alexandria, VA: Association for Supervision and Curriculum Development, 2009.

Karnok, Keith J. "Thoughts on College Teaching." In Stephenson, *Extraordinary Teachers*, 101–14.

Kaufmann, Stephen. *Sabbatical Report on Christian Schools, 2002*. Chattanooga, TN: Covenant College, 2002.

Keliher, Evan. "Forget the Fads—The Old Ways Work Best." *Newsweek*, September 30, 2002.

Keliher, Evan. "If It Wasn't Around in the Middle Ages, It's a Fad." *Education Week* 17, no. 40 (June 17, 1998): 47, 49. www.edweek.org/ew/articles/1998/06/17/40kelihe.h17.html (accessed July 10, 2015).

Lebowitz, Fran. *The Fran Lebowitz Reader*. New York: Vintage, 1994.

Lionni, Leo. *Fish Is Fish*. New York: Dragonfly Books, 1998.

Manning, Brenda H. "Inspiring Students to Excel." In Stephenson, *Extraordinary Teachers*, 133–40.

Marzano, Robert. "Curriculum Design." Presentation at McREL Conference, Kansas City, MO, November 16, 1999.

Marzano, Robert. *The Art and Science of Teaching*. Alexandria, VA: Association for Supervision and Curriculum Development, 2007.

McCann, Thomas M., and Larry R. Johannessen. "Why Do New Teachers Cry?" *The Clearing House* 77, no. 4 (March/April 2004): 138–45.

McKay, Brett, and Kate McKay. "Seneca on the Value of 'Obvious' Advice." *The Art of Manliness*, February 8, 2014. http://www.artofmanliness. com/2014/02/08/manvotional-seneca-on-the-value-of-obvious- advice/ (accessed August 3, 2015).

Mencken, H. L. "Travail." *Baltimore Sun*, October 8, 1928. In *A Mencken Chrestomathy: His Own Selections of His Choicest Writings*, 308. New York: Vintage Books, 1982.

Metzger, Margaret. "Maintaining a Life." *Phi Delta Kappan* 77, no. 5 (January 1996): 346–51.

Morain, Genelle. "Humor as a Welcome Guest in the Classroom." In Stephenson, *Extraordinary Teachers*, 115–24.

Neill, A. S. *Summerhill*. Oxford, UK: Hart Publishing Company, 1960.

Nemerov, Howard. *The Collected Poems of Howard Nemerov*. Chicago: Chicago University Press, 1981.

Palmer, Parker. *Let Your Life Speak: Listening for the Voice of Vocation*. San Francisco: Jossey-Bass, 1999.

Pellicer, Leonard. "Effective Teaching: Science or Magic?" *The Clearing House* 58, no. 2 (October 1984): 53–56.

Postman, Neal. *Technopoly: The Surrender of Culture to Technology*. Visalia, CA: Vintage Press, 1993.

Provost, William G. "The Joys of Teaching English." In Stephenson, *Extraordinary Teachers*, 83–94.

Robinson, Ken. *The Element*. London: Penguin Books, 2009.

Schmoker, Mike. *Focus: Elevating the Essentials to Radically Improve Student Learning*. Alexandria, VA: Association for Supervision and Curriculum Development, 2011.

Segal, Bertie. "Martian Math." Posted on Community TV World forum: http://community.realitytvworld.com/cgi-sys/cgiwrap/rtvw2/commu- nity/dcboard.cgi?az=printer_format&om=22433&forum=DCForu- mID6 (accessed January 24, 2009).

Stephenson, Fred, ed. *Extraordinary Teachers: The Essence of Excellent Teaching*. Kansas City, MO: Andrews McMeel Publishing, 2001.

Stephenson, Fred. "My Teaching Philosophy and the Teachers Who Shaped It." In Stephenson, *Extraordinary Teachers*, 251–61.

Sullo, Bob. *The Motivated Student*. Alexandria, VA: Association for Supervision and Curriculum Development, 2009.

Thomas, Donald. "Education's Seven Deadly Myths." *NASSP Bulletin* 59 (December 1975): 60–66.

Van Dyk, John. *The Craft of Christian Teaching: A Classroom Journey.* Sioux City, IA: Dordt Press, 2000.

Wagner, Tony. "Secondary School Change: Challenge and the Three R's of Reinvention." *Education Week* 22, no. 13 (November 27, 2002): 30, 40.

Weingarten, Gene. "Pearls Before Breakfast." *Washington Post*, April 8, 2007. https://www.washingtonpost.com/lifestyle/magazine/pearls-before-breakfast-can-one-of-the-nations-great-musicians-cut-through-the-fog-of-a-dc-rush-hour-lets-find-out/2014/09/23/8a6d46da-4331-11e4-b47c-f5889e061e5f_story.html (accessed September 23, 2014).

Whitaker, Todd. *What Great Teachers Do Differently.* London: Routledge, 2003.

Wiggins, Grant. "The Case for Authentic Assessment." *Practical Assessment* 2, no. 2 (November 1990). http://ericae.net/pare/110%7Egetvn.html (accessed July 22, 2015).

Wiggins, Grant. "The Futility of Trying to Teach Everything of Importance." *Educational Leadership* 47, no. 3 (November 1989): 44–48, 57–59.

Wiggins, Grant, and Jay McTighe. "Put Understanding First." *Educational Leadership* 65, no. 8 (May 2008): 36–41.

Wilson, Katharine M. "In Praise of Holistic Teaching." In Stephenson, *Extraordinary Teachers*, 227–32.

Wolterstorff, Nicholas. *Educating for Life: Reflections on Christian Teaching and Learning.* Grand Rapids, MI: Baker Academic, 2002.

Wood, George. *A Time to Learn.* New York: Plume, 1999.

About the Author

Scott Holley holds a doctorate in education from Saint Louis University, with his dissertation focusing on the values and philosophies shared by award-winning teachers. He has spent more than forty years in public, international, and private education, earning both the Arlen Dykstra Excellence in Teaching Prize and the Emerson Electric Excellence in Teaching Award. Holley has taught both middle school and high school English, coached basketball, track, and cross country, mentored student teachers through Webster University, and served as both academic dean and interim head of school. He is married, is the father of three, and is the grandfather of three of the most beautiful children in the world.